Ecuadorothy

Ecuadorothy

One Mother and Two Daughters in Ecuador

Dorothy E. Groszhans

(Una Madre Y Dos Hijas En Ecuador)

authorHOUSE®

AuthorHouse™
1663 Liberty Drive
Bloomington, IN 47403
www.authorhouse.com
Phone: 1-800-839-8640

Published by AuthorHouse 10/03/2014

ISBN: 978-1-4969-2550-3 (sc)
ISBN: 978-1-4969-2549-7 (e)

Contents

To my wonderful husband, Mark,
I am eternally grateful for the genetic defect that makes you love me.

To my daughters Carly and Courtney,
Thank you for allowing me to publicly display your eccentricities, all for the sake of money.

(Maybe tens of dollars!)

None of you deserve me.

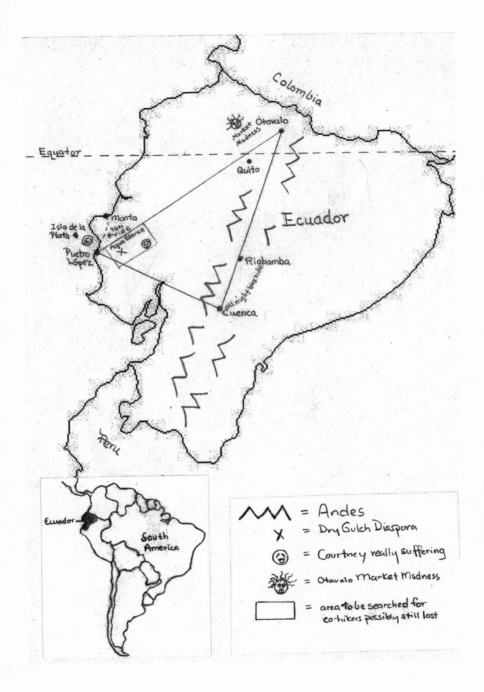

Colombia

Equator

Otavalo
Market
Madness

Quito

Ecuador

Isla de la
Plata

Manta
boat ride

Agua Blanca
✗

Puerto
López

Riobamba

all night bus ride

Cuenca

Peru

Ecuador

South
America

⋀⋀ = Andes

✗ = Dry Gulch Diaspora

🙂 = Courtney really suffering

🌞 = Otavalo Market Madness

▭ = area to be searched for
co-hikers possibly still lost

The lust for comfort kills the passion of the soul.
~ Kahlil Gibran

Fear. That's how I start a journey to a *very foreign* country. Such thoroughly unknown territory makes everything in my comfort zone seem pulled out from under me. I become overwhelmed by the *what ifs. What if* I get sick? Hurt? Kidnapped? *What if* the plane goes down? (Oh, if only we hadn't taken that last seat!) *What if* I'm robbed or get overly tired (that's not fun and I take unflattering photos—that's the worst)? Once again, my daughter Carly makes plans to strike out for the unknown, blazing a trail for the rest of us. She thrives on this kind of adventure—and I get swept along for the ride.

It's a dark and gray winter. Peering around the doorframe of our computer room I see her furiously working the Internet, typing at the speed of light and *making actual commitments* for the summer. This makes me nervous. She is securing a position with a volunteer program, a world organization that is dedicated to elevating the human condition by bringing education to the most remote reaches of the planet. As a 26-year-old teacher, Carly is a prime candidate for these programs, so young, full of energy and enthusiasm to make a positive difference in the world (and she pays them!). She is easily accepted by this organization as a compassionate and committed do-gooder (yeah, sometimes I think she should be committed) and signs up for a four-week program in Otavalo, Ecuador.

By this time, Carly has survived two years of elementary school teaching in our very own high stress/high needs school in a gang-plagued part of town. So, of course, her idea of a summer vacation is to find even higher-needs children, on a physically difficult, oxygen-deprived mountaintop. Well, at least the scenery has potential …

Having visited and lived in any number of (six) Latin American countries, Carly has developed a deep love for their rich and colorful cultures and feels it necessary I should too, broadening my horizons, improving my cultural literacy. So I am included in the master plan. First, she will do-good and then I will come for a ten-day exploratory journey. Faced with my endless excuses as to why it is prudent for me to just stay at home in my comfort zone, Carly only says, "YOU ARE GOING MOTHER!" '

---

*   Though it may sound like I am some kind of *shrinking violet*, I am not. I am basically a Judy Jock but the prospect of being whisked away to such an unknown land and relinquishing all control (especially flying) makes my anticipatory knees quaky.

It's good for me. (Whatever happened to the reasonable, logical mother/ daughter power structure? I think the inversion occurred when Carly had the distinct revelation she was intellectually superior to me in every way—around the age of ten—I was exposed as the parental fraud I knew myself to be.)

The projected trip is to be the summer of 2009 when my youngest daughter, Courtney, is turning twenty-one. We are thinking this would be a pretty *awesome* birthday present for her senior year in college and a valuable lesson learned. In a previous 2005 excursion to Peru and Chile we neglected to include Courtney; it was simply a matter of finances. We have lived to dearly regret this decision, because we are afraid of her and are tired of sleeping with one eye open. (She was very bitter and leans toward violence as a problem-solver.) So this time around we will not make that grievous mistake again—and we can all go back to getting some much needed sleep.

It is easy to know where to begin with this story—vaccinations. No, wait a minute … I should describe the regretful and tragic circumstances of buying our airplane tickets first.

As is usual, with my inherent indecisive temperament, I am loath to commit to any kind of binding decision—hoping instead that all things will just drift down from the ether and miraculously fall into place.' Fortunately, I am surrounded by people not like me. Carly puts on the pressure, "Mother, we need to get our tickets NOW!" You mean plan ahead of time? BY *MONTHS?* With ice in my blood and heel marks scraping the sidewalk, Carly drags me by the armpits into the travel agency. We meet with Rosemary, our lovely Australian agent, inside her chicly cool, white office. She presents us with any number of flying plans, all the while performing a hum of knowledgeable-type-clicking with her highly mysterious computer navigating. Hmmmmm. We weigh our options. It's late Friday afternoon, Carly had a long and tedious work week—her patience is running thin. I suggest we think about it over the weekend (of course), which we do. "Fine! Let's go!" from an exasperated Carly.

---

* It's amazing I ever got married. I would've stayed engaged—a nebulous state of questionable commitment—for an indefinite amount of time.

Oy vey. By Monday, the same tickets went up in price by $300. The cheap seats were gone. ("What other morons are flying to Ecuador in July?" we protested!) For $600 we *could have* booked a fourteen-day excursion—now reduced to a ten-day opportunity at $900. (Is there a lesson here?) I live to sorely regret this penalty of four days. We decide to book before they go up even further.

Now there is the reality of a commitment. Next step, it is essential to get our immunizations for Latin American travel. (Now I am back to the easy place to begin.) We are advised to meet with the International Travel PA (that means *Physicians Assistant* for the less savvy) within our group of medical providers. We schedule a two-hour appointment for the three of us.

It wasn't long enough.

Boosted by Carly's enthusiasm I had steeled myself for the trip by this point—I try to stay calm by self-delusional thinking: *This will probably be a breeze, nothing to worry about—I've done all this before* (the trip to Peru in 2005). But by the end of this marathon of horrors I become completely unraveled.

First of all, I hate the fluorescent lighting and that starchy white, clinical feel while waiting for THE MEDICAL PROFESSIONALS to enter the EXAMINING ROOM (all stressor points for me).* It is a very early seven a.m. and I am not a morning person. A no-nonsense, competent looking duo enter: a young man (this category is getting *older and older* the older I get) and his female training assistant. He is carrying a portable laptop, used to insure that no potential horror about South American travel is overlooked. It is his job to cover the most infinitesimal risks of international travel—and he takes his job very seriously.

So begins our litany of dire warnings. First, his gaze rests upon Carly, as she will be there the longest and therefore the most likely to fatally succumb. Because of her extended stay she will have the most intimate contact with a veritable army of microbial assaults and predatory insects, sharpening

---

* Contrarily, in a foreign country this attention to white sterility makes me feel a lot better.

their little pincers, salivating and ravenous for any unwary gringa, having an especial fondness for extra weak, white ones like her.

On any given trip to Latin America, it is advisable to be current with *all* your basic shots, including those for hepatitis A and B (I always forget which is for what) and tetanus. Because Carly is teaching children, a needle in the arm for *Meningococcal Bacterium* (the word itself strikes fear in my heart—it can't be good—though I'm not sure what it is) is immediately determined. Presto! She is stabbed with a needle. But for a developing world, tropically-based country, nearly every vaccination/inoculation available under the sun seems to be recommended.

Let's start with *typhoid*. To be protected, one has the option to have a "dead vaccine" injected by needle (appealing as it is, the coverage doesn't last as long as *live*); or introduce a "live vaccine" of four doses taken orally every two days, with the vulnerable, Frankenstein-like organism stored in your refrigerator so as not to let it die (a lovely addition indeed to the refrigerator habitat—*careful not get a little typhoid vaccine on your cereal*—can it jump around to other things while it's in there, I wondered.)

Should we be planning to traipse around the tropical portion of Ecuador there's the option of getting a one hundred dollar Yellow Fever vaccine injection (fever spread by a bite from an infected mosquito) as well as needing malaria protection (from a parasite carried by mosquito) for which weeks of pills are required. (We hadn't decided yet about tropical travel, of course.) Were we aware of a new mosquito-borne illness that is insidiously breeding all along the equatorial countries (uh, Ecuador *means equator in Spanish*)? Two bites from this spreading menace can cause internal bleeding? (*Why "two" bites I wonder* ... though I hesitate to interrupt his rapid-fire maelstrom of doom.)

As well-known, diarrheal problems can befall any weakly gringo system when south of the border; but it can get quite serious.* We are advised to take along strong antibiotics in preparation for the worst case scenario. And if that doesn't get us, *altitude sickness* might (we'll often be above 8000

---

* "If you see your mother become incoherent, turn white and stumble, be alarmed." "But mom's always like that ...."

ft, and Carly got desperately ill with *soroche* in Peru); so we may choose to pre-medicate ourselves with several days of pills up to the point of landing. Once we are there, he recommends protecting ourselves with a highly potent DEET insect repellent, suggesting REI in Seattle as a good source for this possible carcinogen. Get regular stuff for Courtney and I, plus a super strength for Carly to be infused into all her clothes. And buy a high strength sunscreen for the equatorial sun (at least 30 SPF—we get 70). While we're at it, he says, purchase water purifying tablets too, it could come in handy. *Why's that?*

I'm not finished. There's a *gnawing* problem of rabid dogs (poor, stray dogs are ubiquitous in South America). Currently there is a worldwide shortage of rabies vaccine so we could not be administered that particular one.[*] Should a stray dog *even lick you*, he advises, we need to seek immediate medical attention or else the consequences could be death within five to seven days of contact. I ask, twice, "Wait a minute. I am a hypochondriac. Are you telling me that *if a dog licks my leg* I have to seek emergency medical attention?" His answers: "Yes," and "Yes." Add to this litany of horrors the Swine Flu epidemic scare currently at its peak.

He leaves the room momentarily to check on our vaccination records. I clearly communicate with my bugged-out eyes, *I'm not going! No one can convince me!* I have an overwhelming urge to flee. *Get me out of here!* The girls wave off my fears. *No big deal.* (Though I know I saw a flicker of fear cross Courtney's eyes.) He returns.

Lastly, he advises purchasing international health insurance. Here's how he states the pros: should you get hijacked they will negotiate the hostage release for you (what a relief). Not only will they locate Western-approved medical facilities as needed, there is the added benefit that they will take care of *shipping your body back home* should things not go well (that would certainly qualify as *not going well*, "Oh, things didn't go very well. Mom's being shipped later.") Apparently, shipping a dead body can be a complicated process that most people don't anticipate. Just when I expect

---

[*] Ironically, Carly met with a couple that had just returned to Yakima from travels in Ecuador. The young woman advised: "The only vaccine I would recommend is the rabies vaccine." Great.

him to assuage my unfounded fears, he begins with the line, "A friend of mine has been living in Quito for two years" (I'm imagining, *and she is just fine, nothing bad ever happened to her*) but instead hear, "and she has been hijacked three times." We all get health insurance called SOS.

For curiosities sake, I inquire, "What if we were going to Europe? What would we have to do?" His direct and simple answer: "Nothing."

And we're going to Ecuador *voluntarily*?

I want to find an enormous sun hat featuring a cascading mosquito net that ties around my ankles.

We three scatter to the wind in different directions after our appointment. I am left with a swirl of information and quaking knees. I weigh my options: The girls can go without me—that's the ticket! No wait, how would that look? I think Ecuador is waaaayyyy too dangerous for me … so I send my daughters? No, that won't work. I can plead my body is too old and can't withstand what youthful (anti)bodies can endure. That's true but doesn't quite cover hijackings and kidnappings. I'll call my sisters, they'll tell me what to do. (Both offered: "DON'T GO!!!") When I ask my husband he thunders, "YOU'RE GOING!" (Hmmmm, what to make of that?) * This was hardly a vacation dilemma like choosing mimosas or margaritas on a beach.

---

* He knows me and my usual pattern: I'm scared. I still go. I have a good experience.

Genetically Shallow

We have a running joke among us traveling females of vanity. I had observed about myself—in the deep recesses of my shallow genetic make-up that, unfortunately, ashamedly, upon perusing the news, whenever a tragedy befell an unusually attractive person I realized (wince) that my sympathetic tendencies were more stimulated than for, say the mundane, average Joe. Yes, I hate to admit this, but it is a scientifically-based human propensity (i.e., teachers unconsciously favor the cute). So in this age of 24-hour-news cycles, before embarking on an overseas adventure, the three of us give some serious thought to the photographs we leave behind. (Courtney retook her passport pics three times.) The girls, displaying an especially cruel strain of sibling rivalry, threaten to post the worst of the worst for the other if left to their own devices. "Ohhh look, how sad that beautiful one is missing. Eh, that other one was probably not going to be happy anyway." It's all in the lighting.

The threat of CNN exposure takes me back to the day of my parenting skills, when the girls were younger. While I would be deeply absorbed in some esoteric endeavor like creating sculptural masterpieces from Supersculpy (bake-in-the-oven clay) or learning Shakespearian put-downs (Take that you untoward knave! *Nooo I've always tried to be a toward knave!*) I would hear an in-motion proclamation from my 16-yr.-old, breezily float past me and out the door, "Mom, I'm going to mumble jumble's house for three weeks." "Okay honey, have a good time … HOLD IT! Whose house? I didn't catch that!"

No, it's not that I'm not conscientious—I am (in a vague sort of way)—and I always naively trust my kids. It was really the threat of an embarrassing lack of details and subsequent exposure should something *untoward* happen:

Hypothetical: Me watching Me on Worldwide CNN:

"Where did she say she was last going ma'am?"

"Um, I dunno, sounded something like Nicole Richie's house."

"When did she say she'd be back?"

"At least in time for graduation … or whenever she felt like it … "

What a complete moron is this disheveled woman!!! (Me Judging Me.)

Hence I run after fleeing daughter, soliciting precise answers through the closed window of her tire spinning, gravel-spitting vehicle. *(That hand gesture wasn't nice Courtney.)*

July 4, 2009

Carly flies off to blaze the trail. (As is customary, whenever Carly—and now Courtney—take off in like manner, their Dad whisks them away in the early morning hours while I, in denial, hold a pillow over my head.) Her flight from Seattle is side-tracked to an unscheduled layover in Panama because, in the seat directly behind Carly, a young woman falls into diabetic seizures and for some reason she is not carrying any needed medications. This results in a seven-hour delay for Carly. In the meantime, I am anxiously waiting to hear from her—watching the clock—to tell me if she arrived safely.

A little after midnight the phone rings. "Mom, I'm in Quito in what I think are the slums. I'm standing on *a sort of* balcony attached to a cinder block building. The hotel name is spray painted on the front wall and I can't read it from here." I would be panicking except for the fact that she is chuckling. Apparently, this program does not have much money to spend on housing volunteers! Fortunately, she feels relatively safe as there are three other volunteers—two young women from England and California, one Australian young man, as well as Stacy, the director (an ex-banker also from England) staying at this hostel as well. She tries to reassure me with this list.

Two noteworthy episodes occurred after we got off the phone. First, unbeknownst to Carly, our phone conversation disturbed a slumbering guest behind a nearby door (who knew?). Bursting out in rage, the sixtyish man bellows at Carly: "I hate all Americans! I just performed a concert and seven Americans ruined my entire performance!" Taken aback, Carly responds in slow deliberation, "So now you hate all Americans …?" "YES!!" shouts the ogreish cellist. "I am now going to politely go back to my bedroom," offers a diffident, receding Carly.

Next, THE BED. After partaking of a chilled shower she pulls back the covers to discover a mass of black hairs. So utterly exhausted she resolves to wrap her beach towel around her body and crashes for a restless night.

9

Dorothy E. Groszhans

July 7

The first photos come rolling in to the family computer back home via e-mail. There she is, on the mountain top, standing before a one room schoolhouse, surrounded by children—and a plethora of potentially rabid dogs.' I scrutinize the photos for any hint of a buffer between her and a lethal lick—but no! She looks euphorically oblivious. She might as well be giving them all puppy kisses! UGH! CARLY!!! The children around her all look ruddy and windswept, and have very serious faces.

Carly's first-hand impressions possess an exhilarating freshness of perspective I couldn't possibly reproduce. Keep in mind, as you read the following correspondence, her menial culinary skills to date peak at "Cheese-Melting on Chips," "Amy's Frozen Vegetarian Dinners," and "Take-Out Restaurants on Speed Dial." This is frightening news this cooking part. (Although hearing of this domestic duty evoked the deepest, sadistic laugh her Dad and I have shared in years. Ditto for extended family and friends.) "Do they know what they've got in Carly?" queried her normally optimistic father.

---

*   At the *tail end* of Carly's tenure, an American medical student (a tall, 22-yr.-old blond girl) along with a couple Quichua nurses randomly showed up at their mountaintop school in a bullhorn equipped van, broadcasting rabies vaccinations for the dogs—summoning the locals to come out and have their dogs treated. This was quite interesting to Carly because all the families hitherto unseen came pouring out of their huts. The method was nearly comical as the dogs were stuck helter-skelter with needles—one dog taking off with an embedded needle in its backside.

A bullhorn affixed to the top of a vehicle is a common sight and sound in Latin America—used to notify of water or gas deliveries, for instance, or political agendas, often projecting a melodious tune to gain your attention. Ironically, in my previous writings about Peru I had fictitiously used the Clint Eastwood theme song from "The Good, The Bad and The Ugly" as a backdrop to one of my imagined scenes of peril: lo and behold, when Carly was staying in Puebla, Mexico, what does she hear coming down the street but that very same haunting, whistling tune. "MOTHER, you won't believe this!" she phones.

10

Hola todos,

I don't know where to begin, I'm having such an amazing experience. I'm teaching on top a misty mountain that overlooks other volcanoes and mountains in *Huayrapungo* which means "where the wind blows through" and let me tell you it does!

We teach in a little blue school house and the kids come from all around to attend school and get food. They even catch our van up the hill, running after it to tell it to stop! We also take indigenous women back down to the market; it was so amazing to have them in the bus chatting in Quichua wearing their beautiful dresses, very other worldly! It takes about an hour to get up there on a dusty, very bumpy road which has been blocked so far by the following: horses, cows, pigs, dogs, children herding, and indigenous women and girls carrying packs on their backs. The views along the way are astounding, especially at 7 a.m. and at 9,000 feet altitude! The kids are gorgeous in their indigenous attire, especially the girls with their colorful dresses and abundant jewelry. When we first arrive we go into a very antiquated rusty kitchen and take out huge pots to cook oats for the kids. I also had to light the gas stove today ... that was very exciting! AAAAh! And can you believe I'm in charge of cooking everyday (with another volunteer from the USA who also never cooks). We make them soup for lunch in an enormous pot with an equally enormous spoon.

This Monday and Tuesday I taught six students ranging in age from 14 to 19. They were really fun, sweet and diligent. They laughed hard at my pathetic attempts to draw animals ... everything was a circle body, circle head, and 4 stick legs. I ended up just acting them out! We even have some parents show up, who are so humble and brave to start their education now with their children. They also were willing to do all my songs I do with the second graders in the USA. Everyone around the world loves the song "Bananas!" Wednesday, Thursday, and Friday I will teach younger kids in Spanish in the morning and English fun activities in the afternoon ... we'll see how it goes!

I feel so honored to have this unique experience. I have to go and plan lessons for tomorrow with the other volunteers, who come from all over, England, Australia, USA, Norway, Denmark, and Sweden. A guy from Australia lives in my house with me but I only understand about

11

25 percent of what he says, but he looks like Russell Crowe so it's not too bad, I just nod my head and try to laugh when appropriate ....

Ahh I'm late to go lesson plan, talk to y'all later! Oh, my host family is really great and sweet and Otavalo is such an intriguing colorful market town with mountains in the distance in every direction!

Adios,
Carlita

You can't imagine the fearful image cast in our heads of Carly—imbecilic even at striking a match—lighting a volatile gas stove each morning. ("OPEN ALL THE DOORS AND WINDOWS FIRST!" WE BESEECHED!) On this stove she prepared daily a witch-sized black caldron full of *needing-to-be-cooked* meat and vegetables to serve her students. I don't know who was most at peril! One of the first Quicha words she learned was from this perplexing, vociferous outcry from all her students at lunchtime: "Kachi! Kachi! Kachi!" ("Salt! Salt! Salt!") only to have one little guy push his chair, crawl on top of a table and lift himself up to the adult-height cupboard (all to the students' strident chorus of kachi! kachi! kachi!) to retrieve the salt stash for all his classmates. (In the process revealing some noticeable toddler-cheek as the string holding up his oversized, hand-me-down pants wasn't up to the job.)

As a long-time vegetarian, she was also in charge of buying the school's food supplies each week at Otavalo's open-air food market—including graphically displayed butcher shops for the meat portion of the soup. Perusing an outdoor meat market showcasing fresh flesh specialties like severed calf's leg with hair (have photo to prove), skinned *cuy* (guinea pig with teeth intact), pig stomach or other various intestines, is a vegetarian's nightmare! About as far away as you can get from a tofu hot dog. (It's amazing what you can do when you have to.) The teachers were instructed *never* to partake of the food they served to the students as they could get quite ill from the foreign ingredients (as Carly's co-volunteer from Virginia learned the hard-retching way), never to eat in front of the students, nor to leave any remnants of food or garbage on the premises as the children tend to snatch and consume it.

Meanwhile, back home …

So here we are, getting photos and updates of what seems a most exotic adventure. In a strange twist we here in Washington State are experiencing

---

* When we visited the local meat market and it was indeed startling. I recall an open, plastic crate of bloody things (intestines?) being kicked along the grungy sidewalk right next to me.

a record-breaking heat—an unheard of three digits in Seattle—while Carly is *cooling off* near the equator! So far the temperatures in her Andean Highlands home (elevation of Otavalo city is at 8441 feet) have been averaging in the mild seventies—kind of a pyramid temperature graph each day: very cold mornings, mid-afternoon sunburst (remove sweaters and scarves) followed by cold nights. We are to experience the same weather pattern as she when we arrive four weeks later: cozy candlelit restaurants and a welcome fire at night were blissful and kind of bizarre considering the circumstances we had just left in Seattle. However, when the sun did break through the ever-hovering, turbulent clouds, usually by mid afternoon, the rays were quite intense.

Ongoing Phone Updates to Home

7/5 I am glad to hear that she is now safely ensconced with her host family in Otavalo—a young *mestizo* couple with three small children. And she's got her own clean little room! Yay!

* Their six-year-old son helped her unpack and thoroughly enjoyed listening to Trisha Yearwood's "Wrong Side of Memphis" on Carly's iPod.

* A young Australian guy is staying there too … same age and apparently cute like Russell Crowe. (I told Carly to *tell him* to lock his door at night.)

* Her biggest worry is that she will be **working very hard** from the get-go. They are thrilled to have an actual teacher! Today, around 7 a.m. they were to buy groceries for the students before they head out to the remote location. They are warned never to leave any food waste behind because the children will eat it. Am anxious to hear how her first day of work goes!

7/6 Okay, so her first day teaching (unfortunately Mark took the call while I was out walking and this is what I forced out of our nonverbal male):

* She had a great day. There is no village at the end of the dirt road to the school; it is just a small building on a hill. She will teach two sessions: one with nine children and two adults (parents) and one with ten teenagers. Apparently the free food is a big draw.

* The school is hoping Carly can write their entire curriculum because she is an actual teacher (a little panic here, she has only two years experience) emphasizing science and math! (Not her expertise.)

* Courtney and I will not be able to see where she's teaching; it is not allowed.

* The sun comes up at 6:30 a.m. and sets at 6:30 p.m. Every day. Because of their location on the equator.

* She was happy with the delicious dinner her host family cooked the previous night: fried bananas and "some kind of potato" soup.

7/8 What I learned in a long phone conversation ($$$) around 8 p.m. (10 p.m. for her):

* The rickety old van that takes them up the hill constantly stops for tiny children that seem to come out of nowhere, flagging it down to get to school. Once the kids get on the van they cheerfully sit on laps—all dressed in colorful native clothes. However, many of them have multiple sores from living in such harsh, high altitude conditions. She commonly sees the teeniest toddlers wandering about, teetering on precipices by themselves, or supervised by an older five-year-old sibling.

* A woman that lives in a hut near the school has eight children; the father left them destitute. Apparently, the food the school provides is their only reliable food source.

* Dust from the constant wind makes it hard, if not impossible, to stay clean, from self-hygiene to the school kitchen. Both Carly and her co-volunteer from Virginia are kitchen-challenged—even though the co-volunteer has already worked there for seven weeks.

* It's so funny to think of the children *and the parents* enjoying Carly's "Bananas" song-and-dance routine (all for the sake of learning English). Everyone pantomimes *being a banana*, unpeeling themselves while chanting the song together: hand thrusts "chop bananas, chop, chop bananas"then the shoulder-shimmying "shake bananas, shake, shake bananas" etc. I can just see them all singing and giggling together just as Carly described, the adult women especially tickled. (Ecuador is one of the worlds major sources of bananas too! with at least fifty varieties—tiny finger ones to short fat red ones.)

* A source of my motherly worry (besides Carly lighting the gas stove) is that bathing involves the use of an "electrical shower" as Carly puts it. Sparks are flying throughout the duration. *What?* (More details later.)

* She is really enjoying the companionship of the other volunteers in the program, all 20-somethings from England, Sweden (specifically Småland, from whence our ancestors emigrated), Switzerland and Australia. They all went out last night and Carly had them laughing pretty hard with her attempt at a British accent. *Cheerio maties!*

General e-mail correspondence from Carly to family and friends:

I feel so passionate about the work I'm doing here. It is wonderful that there are organizations like this to try to ameliorate the gross inequities that exist in the world. It is shocking to see so many children working. It is incredible what they are expected to do at such a young age. On the way up to the school there are so many children herding, picking, and carrying their younger siblings on their backs. This morning a Quichua woman sat next to me with her two young children wrapped in the front and back. It was so astounding for me to look at her, probably in her 30s but looking much older, and realizing that we live on this same planet but our lives are so drastically different. Even in comparison to the people in the city, like my host family, their lives are starkly different. *Notthatonewayoflivingisbetterthananother*, living in the country should be lovely, but they should also have the same opportunities. – Carly

Three Weeks In: Carly's Personal Notes From The Field

Here are some random things that I need to write down or I will forget.

* A student rode to school this week on his horse!

* Many showers here (for bathing) are electric … it is terrifying, who thought of that anyway?

* Many of my students didn't show up this week because they were harvesting potatoes; you can see these little colorful dots all over the hills of people picking potatoes.

* I go with the kids on many "Quichua English" walks where the kids tell me the words of things in Quichua and I tell them the word in English. So cool! The kids are so smart; they are going to know three languages! But unfortunately they are considered stupid in town, which makes me so mad because they know so much more and have had to work so hard. Many of these situations remind me of my immigrant students at home, just not as extreme as here. I finally bought some baby wipes with aloe and vitamin E so I can clean their poor marked little faces from the cold high altitude temperatures and the bitter wind. The project doesn't want to get involved in medical issues because it would be too overwhelming, which I understand, but you can't just leave the kids with skin infections that are bleeding …

* Electricity going out in house. I had to crawl on my knees and go find the baby who was crying upstairs, as my four-year-old host brother was holding on to my back.

* I am considered an "expert" here in teaching and ESL so the director had me give a workshop this week to all the other volunteers because I'm one of the only teachers with an ESL background that speaks Spanish. I taught them a lot of songs and games I learned from the summer camps in Italy to try and make it fun! The director said that it is so great to bring some fun and laughter into the children's lives. Many of the students here work all week and then the older ones even go to weekend school. They don't have the opportunity to play and just be kids very often.

* Waiting for the van at 7 a.m. I saw one of my eight-year-old students waiting there for the van too. I looked all around for an adult family member but to my shock he had to come down all by himself at who-knows-what hour to go to the market to buy food for his family and somehow knew where to find us. I'm so amazed at what little kids do here ... I've seen two of my female students (12- and 14-years old) come to class with infants wrapped up on their backs. I even see girls who look no more than six carrying their little siblings. They all take care of each other though, it is very sweet. I also see so many LITTLE kids on the way up the mountain herding the farm animals, carrying food, it never ceases to be shocking, sad, and incredible at what kids are capable of when they have to ... it is so hard to realize that the lives of many children in the world are like this.

* We often give many of the families rides back to town or up to the village. Some of the poor Quichua women have to hear us sing all the way up and own the mountain. Our van driver, José, has the most random mix of music. We found a "Savage Garden Greatest Hits" and went crazy singing as loud as we could up the mountain. Actually by "we" I mean this other crazy American and I who dance and serenade everyone else. I guess we're not breaking any loud American stereotypes, but how can you not sing to "All By Myselffffffff" and "Truly Madly Deeply." I even got José to sing the "oooo aaaaah" parts with my water bottle microphone. When we picked up the other volunteers on Friday, who have to hike back from their school, we were on top of the van singing, "I want to stand with you on a mountain ...." It was so hilarious, at least to us. When can you sing Savage Garden at full blast out the window at 7 a.m. on your way up a mountain in Ecuador?

* It has been so much fun hanging out with the other volunteers from around the world, including Denmark, Sweden, and Norway, and they speak English perfectly! We make fun of our accents all the time and at our attempts to mimic them, or maybe they are just laughing at me trying to do *cheerio maties*. But I've almost got it!

My body is so sore from hiking ten hours in the middle of nowhere with my "host uncle" Erick, who is 26. It was amazing to see where he and my host mom, Rosa, grew up. My mouth almost dropped open when we finally reached his parents' shack on a hill, far into backcountry. I felt like

I was traveling back in time to see how my great, great, great grandparents lived. They had a dirt floor kitchen where all the food is homemade. Miles away from any hospital, grocery store, or *anything* they are basically self-sufficient. She gave birth to *all eight of their children* in this home. It was astounding to see where Rosa and Erick grew up because now they seem so modern!

It actually looked like a fun place for children to grow up, running free and playing with all the animals but Erick says he hated it and couldn't understand why I was so fascinated. At the age of ten they had to walk to Ibarra, two hours away, for school. Erick used to hike all over these mountains and knew all the trails. He said that his dad would walk barefoot and even carried his sick father all the way into town.

I was doing really well the first five hours of the journey, but I had no idea that there were five more hours to go on a "trail" that only Erick had used and created—the last time four years ago. There were bugs, snakes, lizards, and brambles everywhere. I fell three times and twisted my knee and got scrapes everywhere. At one point I didn't get up and almost cried. The other side of the hill was rainy and lovely, but on the way down it changed to desert. My legs and knees hurt so badly from going straight down for four hours, and all I could see—far, far away—was a tiny village that we had to reach by 6:30 p.m. to catch a bus—or else had to walk some more. I couldn't believe that Erick had walked up and down this a hundred times as a kid.

Finally, I hobbled into the settlement, covered in dirt and scrapes with tears in my eyes. It was only a little pueblo but it seemed like civilization at last! Everyone was hanging out on a Saturday night, barbequing downtown and playing cards—it looked like an old town from the Wild West. They all stopped and just *starrrrrrrrred* at me! To them it must've seemed like a strange gringa just popped out of the sky! Erick said I was probably the first gringa *ever* to hike that trail! (He even carved my name into an aloe plant to mark the occasion!)

Next we had to catch a truck (hitchhike) down the rest of the hill and then catch two buses for the three-hour ride back to Otavalo. I thought I'd never get back to my bed. It seemed thousands of mosquitoes had bitten my dirt-caked, scraped skin. Erick abandoned me halfway through the bus ride for his home, leaving me for the last hour by myself. I had *no idea* where to get off, but fortunately he had instructed the driver to let me know, and thank goodness he did because I was so exhausted I fell asleep. Dizzily, I descended off the bus in the dark—very turned around—and had to walk one mile back to the house. I finally stumbled in the door, looking like a crazy woman! Rosa was aghast, "Ahhh I can't believe you walked all that way!" She herself *had never* taken that path because it was far too difficult! I took a shower, ate everything, and slept until 12:30 p.m. the next day. I certainly look at her differently now, knowing her exotic history. I am amazed at the vast difference between city life and country life.

I can't believe I only have a week left to work, and then I will see Mom and Courtney and travel around for ten days. I will be sad to leave even though it is so much work; it is such an experience of a lifetime. I love the town I'm staying in, maybe I will come back someday. I've never had time go so fast, probably because I'm working so hard. I think I'm going to have reverse culture shock when I come home.

High Andes hilltop school: *Huayrapungo* "where the wind blows through"

Carly with two of her four- and five-yr.-old students and their mother. (Shown here with three of her eight sons who live nearby).

Protecting from the wind.

Students helping with harvest (next to school)

Processing legumes

Sorting crop

23

Teaching yoga (The Tree Pose) to her high school students.

Carly cooking lunch for the students

With Luis near school

Carly's co-volunteer, a 21-year-old college student from Vermont, was experiencing burn-out after ten weeks isolation at this mountaintop school. One day, while the children were busy coloring, she concocted a menu of suicide options (tongue-in-cheek) that looked something like this.

"The hottest weather occurred from July 26 to August 2, 2009 … with the peak high of 103 °F (39 °C) at Seattle-Tacoma International Airport on **July 29** set the record for the hottest temperature **ever** in Seattle since records began in 1894."[1]

July 29

My husband, Mark, drives us from Yakima's sweltering 104 degrees, 150 miles west to Seattle's 103 degrees—to cool off—and to take Courtney and me to the airport to catch our next day 6 a.m. flight. Do you think I am nervous and apprehensive? Mentally I go over every item packed for the flight, ad nauseam—and then again in our hotel room. I physically unpack, repack, semi-pack, mock pack, kinda pack—several times; then check for my: passport, yellow vaccination record, credit card, extra money, driver's license and airplane tickets in their secret khaki hideaway pouch (hidden beneath my shirt) that no mugger could ever be so savvy as to spot. ("Let's see," surmises the would-be thief: "An obvious tourist with khaki strap around her neck with an equally obvious bulge protruding at her mid-drift—occasionally accompanied by suitably matching and bulging offspring. Clearly, it's just a strange manifestation of familial chubbiness and not hidden valuables!" He leaves us alone.)

ADVANCED WARNING: A peek inside my brain:

WHAT IF I LOSE MY CREDIT CARD! MY PASSPORT! MY PACK! MY MEDICATIONS (okay, they're not life-sustaining, but still … my cholesterol would go up). I IMAGINE THE SURLY FACES OF PASSPORT AGENTS—mustachioed, armed and sweaty—and these are the women—SHAKING THEIR HEADS IN SULLEN DISAPPROVAL WHEN I CAN'T PRODUCE MY PASSPORT. "YOU ARE SENTENCED TO SPEND THE ENTIRE TEN DAYS IN BAD FLOURESCENT LIGHTING, DISMAL WAITING ROOMS, AND NEEDLESSLY LONG LINES WHILE THIS MATTER IS INCOMPETENTLY HANDLED … " "AND COCAINE IS SURREPTIOUSLY PLANTED ON YOUR PERSON … if we feel like it." Heads thrown back in unison, revealing a morass of substandard dental work around quivering tonsils, they laugh in cruel and mocking merriment, happy their work tedium has suddenly been lifted at the expense of this dumb gringa. I look over only to see my backpacked-children give me a dour look of disappointment now that I've wrecked everyone's trip. (Followed by a "See ya' in ten," by Courtney.)

WHAT IF I DON'T BRING ENOUGH UNDERWEAR AND SOCKS!!!

I send Mark and Courtney to dinner without me—and to buy extra socks. Because we are carrying everything on our backs and above all want to be as mobile as possible, I am haunted by a PBS TRAVEL EXPERT's advice ricocheting about my head, ping, ping, ping: "Take out everything *you think* you'll need and put half of it back." So I did. In the middle of our trip I wanted to kill that woman.ᐟ

SEATTLE'S TEMPERATURE SKYROCKETS as the air conditioner blasts in our hotel room. Occasionally, I look down from the moisture-condensed windows of our third-floor room to the Marriott Courtyard's atrium and aqua-colored swimming pool. I envy the carefree little people having a good time while I engage in obsessive-compulsive behavior. Later, as I myself sit poolside among the tropical flora, I muse, "This artificial paradise is so beautiful, why do we have to go to the real thing? I don't get it. I'm not seeing even one creepy-crawly thing (except that man who shouldn't be wearing a Speedo) and it's all so sterile and safe—no death-dispensing microbes lurking in the bougainvillea, preparing to fell me!"

But I still have one last minute errand to accomplish. During a four-month-ago, Spring shopping trip to Seattle's premier Outdoor Recreation Store (REI)—to get those doctor recommended mega-force insect repellents— Carly and Courtney stumbled upon THE PERFECT TRAVELING PANTS for our trip: soft, durable, space age material, easy to clean AND they converted from pants to shorts with the ease of a zip. Hanging over my shoulder, tightly attended and scrutinized by Courtney, all the while shopping for travel clothes, she could not tolerate the thought that I should

---

*   All right, I didn't take out that much and it has a happy ending. I was forced to buy cool, light weight pants, suitable for a tropical climate, to replace the clothes I had removed. I really love those pants. Courtney got some too. We briefly felt like natives.

have similar attire (though different colors and even brands) as she and Carly—insisting that I save money and make use of a cotton pair I had bought some hundred years ago.[*]

Well, despite her protests—and luck of an REI near our airport hotel—I was determined not to be denied this second chance! I made my way to the store with Mark (he had to drive his company vehicle or I'd have gone solo) and bought TWO expensive pairs! (He will buy just about anything to escape prolonged shopping. I know this.) Dang if Courtney wasn't semi-right. I was very glad I had them (those cottons would've been a mucky disaster) but with our limited supplies we had to negotiate *daily* on who got to wear what (always a crabby procedure) so that we weren't triplets. On some days it was impossible to achieve disparity. I'll leave it there.

Smug in the air: Courtney dragged her beige khaki-clad leg right across a blackened tailpipe early on in the trip—and it cleaned up like a charm. I happily pointed out the wisdom of us *all* buying the superior material. *That hand gesture to your mother wasn't nice Courtney.*

---

* "Noooo mother, *you* do not need those expensive items ... but I do!" Reminds me of the comment she made, as I prepared for a fun trip to New York last year in which she, for lack of money, couldn't go. "But your time is over!" she stamped.

Imagined Kidnap Negotiations

So when it comes down to it, just what paltry sum are we worth should the unthinkable happen?

Kidnapper's phone call to our home: "How much are you willing to pay to get (the entire financial burden of) your family back?"

Husband Mark: "Is this a joke?"

Kidnapper: "¡Señor! I don't think you understand the seriousness of the situation!"

Mark: "I don't think you understand you kidnapped an average American family. Do you have any idea how in debt we are? Are we talking any rebates here?"

Kidnapper: "Let's get down to it! How much cold, hard cash can you send?"

Mark: "I'll have to check the car floors and all the coat pockets before I answer."

Kidnapper: "¡SEÑOR!"

Mark: "All right, all right. This is difficult to determine: The youngest one still has a year to go at an expensive private college. The old one (me) has always landed me in the poverty column of the tax brackets—that's kinda helpful. The middle one pays rent, so she's worth something to me."

Kidnapper: "¡AY!" Muy rápido: **"De todos los turistas americanos en el mundo y nosotros tienen que secuestrar a la familia de Bundy del Al!!!"** ("Of all the American tourists in the world and we have to kidnap the Al Bundy family!!!")

Mark: "I'm pretty busy watching basketball right now. Can you call me back later?"

While Carly translates the ensuing negotiations for us—the content provoking our shocked disbelief—the tawdry cost analysis drags on. (And I am so regretting the nagging e-mail I sent Mark earlier.)

Mark (chomping on an illicit Ho-Ho donut) dreamily contemplates life without us: twenty-four-seven freedom to watch *never-ending sports play-offs* on his now affordable, big screen TVs in every room; refrigerator stocked with heaps of blueberry pies; and no one to push him out the door to exercise or to make him eat broccoli or Brussels sprouts *ever again*. But wait! (the saving grace), he realizes that after a few days of his adult Home Alone fantasy it's not really that much fun when there's no one around to out-wit and out-maneuver—his lifelong perfected tactics instantly become worthless!

Mark: "Can you at least keep them for a few extra days before I send the money?"

ME: "HAND ME THAT TELEPHONE."

---

* Like the skill of feigning 25 viruses (I marked them on the calendar) one winter, severe enough to require much rest and TV sports watching.

AT LAST, at the stroke of four a.m. Mark has the distinct pleasure to ~~get~~ ~~rid of~~ deposit us at the Sea-Tac airport. He quickly, anxiously, assists me through a bewildering (to me) maze of airport procedure—that now includes self-serving computer technology (stressor!). All checked-in! Why is there a look of relief on his face as we approach the metal detector … and a hint of a smile? In a nanosecond he disappears from view. I crane my neck to spot him, but he has taken off. *Where'd he go so quickly? We're not even through the gate yet!* Could it be the pull of uninterrupted ESPN Sports Channel and eating whatever he likes with no observant wife *guiding him along* (relentlessly) that makes him so eager to rush off? Good thing I asked my sisters to do surprise spot checks on him in my absence!

Once on the plane, I relinquish all control to Fate … and some to my seemingly cool and competent daughter. Finally, I've done all I can—there's some relief in thinking *well it's just too late now*—we're on our way. Let's see: I've got my headphones, blow-up neck pillow (nerdy says Carly), healthy nut snacks, self-indulgent magazine, the *New York Times*, eye mask and baseball cap (so no one can see me sleeping), extra clothes in case I get cold, and a journal—does it get any better than this? So efficient and self-contained! I LOVE IT!*

The only fly in the ointment, so to speak, is the tragic human condition to be just like every animal on the planet. Occasionally I have to crawl over and disturb two previously comfy people (I always have a window seat) to go the bathroom. I hate this. In a perfect world, why can't there be a "Vacation-Cessation Pill"—a short term suspension of all bodily fluids until one is comfortably back home? I don't know how this would work without looking like a Macy's Parade inflated balloon at the end of a vacation (*is that mom billowing down the exit ramp?*)—but it would sure make traveling a lot more pleasant!

Landing in Atlanta, it's the little things that bring joy. I love the hustle and bustle and drama of airport terminals bringing together travelers from *all over the world*—and I am one of them! I am never happier than

---

* Except for taking off. When I was younger I LOVED FLYING— it was like a fun carnival ride, so adventurous. Something fundamental has changed in my 56-yr.-old body. Now all I can think about are news footage depicting horrific crashes. I close my eyes and brace myself for the agonizing thrust. Aaaaaggghhhh!

when—especially after I've been denied access—I have a long-deserved giant vat of Starbucks coffee in my hands (regular drip with cream, the cream being a sin for my cholesterol) and Hudson's Newsstands at my fingertips. NOW the adventure begins!!! Woo Hoo! I'm caffeine buzzing all over the place, trying not to irritate an irritable Courtney with my new found, artificially-induced, enthusiasm! !!! !! !

By the time we reach our destination (16 hours of travel) *we are weary*. It is unbelievable to us that within one day's travel time, we can go from the northernmost U.S. to San Francisco de Quito, Ecuador. Almost like entering a black hole and coming out at a different place and time in the universe. We know as our plane is approaching that Carly and her Ecuadorian host *Javier* (lucky for us he is a cab driver by profession) are awaiting our arrival. They have driven nearly two hours from Otavalo only to have our flight arrive at ten p.m.—two hours late. From the airplane, we look down at the mysterious, rolling hills of Quito's golden city lights (at least 1.5 million people) that seem to stretch into infinity—every single available spot of land inhabited. The plane tilts sideways towards the airstrip; the adrenal rush of the airplane's roar at descent heightens the excitement of our arrival.

Bleary-eyed, we go through the necessary prerequisites before gaining admittance to a foreign country—horribly long queues for everything as usual. But here everyone is required to don white surgical face masks—Ecuador's precaution against the current Swine Flu scare. This is a little disconcerting. Are they protecting us or the airport personnel? Next to me are some medical students who scoff at this attempt—explaining that wearing a mask will do nothing of the sort. As I look up I see a glass-encased crowd peering down at us from an overhead room and Carly jumping up and down in excitement! Wow, I'm surprised she could pick us out amongst a room seemingly full of surgical assistants.

So this is how we enter Ecuador.

It's amazing to see Carly again in this foreign environment—though she looks thoroughly acclimated. Finally exiting from the somewhat shabby airport (my hasty observation), ripping our masks off and standing in the brisk night air, we are formally introduced to Carly's "host dad," Javier. He is a nice looking, clean-shaven 32-year-old *mestizo* (mixed Spanish and Indian descent), dark hair, slender build and average height. Carly explains that in an act of respect to me, THE ESTEEMED MADRE, Javier sports a new haircut and a newly washed taxi/car (and lots of nervous apprehension). Even a mustache was sacrificed in my honor! That is so sweet! I try to ease his misdirected tension about me by laughing a lot. No, I am no overbearing *mamacita!* Quite the contrary. If anything my kids bear over me.

We pile into his aged, mostly seatbelt-less vehicle' with windows that don't roll down in the back (I tried). First of all, to exit the parking lot, we have to pay at a gated stop *two whole dollars* for four hours of parking. Shockingly cheap. (It is fortunate and convenient *for us* that Ecuador switched to the dollar in 2001—though Javier says that the conversion was a financial disaster for the locals and many saw their life savings plummet in value.)

---

* Only on the **rare occasion** were we ever treated to a seatbelt in Ecuador. In one taxi, I *tried* to pull them out of the crevices—I could see it was equipped—until, unsuccessful and thoroughly exasperated, I gave up. "Carly, ask him how to access these!" Translation: "He says that he got the car cleaned once and the seatbelts got stuck below. He never bothered to get them out again." Unbelievable.

Otavalo

A Long and Winding Road

It is a tiring two-hour journey before we ever reach Javier's home. Carly is kept busy translating from the front seat as I make feeble attempts at Spanish from the back, like: *Que pasa cerveza?* (What's happening beer?) Javier, good-naturedly, laughs a lot—as we all do. Carly is sooooo excited to finally be able to show us her world! Javier finds it amusing, puzzling in fact, that I am so thrilled to actually be traveling on THE PAN-AMERICAN HIGHWAY—about which I have read so many South American adventure stories.

A gibbous moon lights the landscape as I strain to take in the environs. The miles we travel on the Pan-American Highway to Otavalo are over mostly unpopulated mountainous terrain, interspersed with infrequent, sprawling settlements. The dwellings I observe from the car are nothing like I had expected. Thus far the characteristic Spanish-style adobe or native constructed mud-brick dwellings are few and far between. Mostly I catch sight of bland structures made up of heavy, gray, concrete slabs—many in a state of partial construction—that remind me of old news footage I've seen of Soviet Union state-sponsored housing. This flat horizontal structure is neither appealing nor interesting. From the roadside view, there is an overriding pall of poverty. Javier's explains that the *indígenas* take a long time to build some of these homes; construction limps along with available funds. Occasionally, I spot a prosperous looking tiled and adobe home, isolated with its own hilltop view—hmmmm, I wonder where that money comes from?

We have to stop twice along remote stretches of the highway to pay road tolls at massively flood-lit, intimidating, and multi-gated checkpoints. Courtney has fallen asleep by this time, lying against me in the backseat as I study armed guards standing at the wayside. *What are they for?*

It is closing in on one a.m. when we finally turn into Javier's driveway. Actually, it is not a driveway at all but a gated patio he must first unlock and then *tightly squeeze* his car through. He pulls into a negligible space, right against their front door. Their residence is part of a walled compound consisting of three families and several dogs that share a central courtyard. As usual, at first impression, I am shocked by where Carly is living—the living conditions seem well below standard to me. Though I quickly adjust I'm thinking, *Why do they have to be so tightly locked up? What is the danger lurking in this neighborhood?*

Though Carly and I had protested for weeks ahead, Javier and his wife, Rosa, insist on giving up their bedroom for me. I would be just fine in their spare room, but once again "Madre reverence" reigns. I thank him profusely and Courtney and I drag our luggage up the narrow, creaky wooden stairs to bed.

I am touched by the neatly arranged throw pillows, the threadbare soft blankets on the bed—everything is quite modest, but it is clear that much care has been taken. The bedroom is large: exposed wooden beams cross the ceiling, a worn couch sits against a far window, and, as typical, one bare light bulb (circular low-energy type) dangles from an exposed wire in the ceiling. There are no reading lamps.

Even in my stupefied state, the color scheme seems a bit bizarre to me. (In fact we laugh with Rosa, who brings it up the next day, as she describes her husband's predilection for odd color pairings as *loco*.) In our master bedroom, one wall off the sitting area is a baby blue that juts onto the mustard-yellow wall of the sleeping area. (And Carly's bedroom is pink.) It seems incongruous with the organic nature of the adobe building. But, *que sé yo?* (What do I know?)

We, thankfully, have our own little bathroom too. However, here my memory is refreshed about a common *south of the border* detail: YOU CANNOT PUT TOILET PAPER IN THE TOILET! (I had forgotten about this from other travels—their infrastructure simply can't handle it.) There is always a waste basket provided; I will say no more. Their fashionable sink is adorable, but doesn't function at all. We have to brush our teeth in the bathtub which is continually occupied by a congregation of slender, wiggly insects.

Thoroughly exhausted, Courtney and I crash in our double bed around two a.m. Poor Carly has to work one last day and leaves bright and early the next morning at six. We will be left to fend for ourselves in this strange, new environment!

Starting around five a.m. a lusty rooster begins its piercing, relentless, summons to rise through our open window. Dogs bark, chickens cluck, it is all we can do to keep falling back to sleep between abrupt interruptions. Finally, around nine a.m., I hear this sweet voice coming up the stairs, "Dor a thé, Dor a thé, it is time for breakfast." It is Javier using his very limited English. I respond courteously, "Oh, yes, thank you. I'll be right down." Though a slumbering Courtney refuses to rise with me! This is a big problem. I know about five words of Spanish; at least Courtney has a rudimentary knowledge. I continue to attempt coaxing, but *no deal!* I am the only one to bravely venture downstairs.

It is clear Rosa and Javier are nervous about hosting the Mamacita! I mistakenly think I will be able to communicate simply with kind gestures. I am very wrong. Though I can't verbally express myself, I can see my constant smiling and laughing helps ease the tension and they soon realize their fears about me are unfounded. They can relax.

I have brought gifts for the household: a crank-generated flashlight (there are frequent power failures) and a doll of dark complexion for their little girl (as opposed to all the blonde-haired Barbie types). The gifts are a big hit, especially the doll. However, I can barely communicate ANYTHING (for example, how to operate the still-packaged flashlight or that it has a magnet for hanging on the refrigerator), virtually none of my gestures translate—no matter how hard I try or they try. It is verrrrry awkward! I'm beginning to perspire. Finally, thankfully, after about 25 minutes of this, Courtney descends from the upstairs bedroom and is able to translate for us. Whew! All that pressure is finally off me! Once Courtney solves our language-barrier mysteries, we have a lovely time chatting at the breakfast table. Courtney reluctantly translates for me: "You are not at all what they expected. So nice, youthful and cute." From this I decide I love them.

On a gas stove, slinging ten month-old daughter, Luz, on her hip, Rosa cooks breakfast. She serves us very salty eggs, fried potatoes, some bread, instant Nescafé, and a thick fruit drink called a *batido*—today it is a mixture of papaya and milk though *batidos* (*batido* means *beaten*) can be made from many fruit combinations. A plastic tablecloth covers the wooden table where we sit in a small dining alcove, near a window. The dim and somewhat dank kitchen, right off the dining area, is lit by a glaring, bare, energy-efficient light bulb. Though I understand the fluorescent bulb is an economic necessity, the effect is harsh.

Rosa is an attractive, 34-year-old woman of *mestizo* descent, just as her husband Javier is of Spanish and Indian heritage. I am intrigued by her choice of clothing: navy blue sweat pants and sweat shirt, she looks just like any Western college student. They have two rambunctious little boys (ages six and four) and their adorable cherub-cheeked little girl. The sons sporadically pop up and down, laughing, behind a living room couch as we eat in the adjoining breakfast room.

We are so very grateful for their kindness and hospitality, knowing they are under tremendous financial pressure to make ends meet. (We paid for the night's lodgings with them rather than give the money to a local hotel). The minute Carly vacated her room the next day—her four week stint as a volunteer over—a new boarder from England arrived immediately.

Rosa shows us around her home. I am surprised to find luxurious, forest green, leather couches and chairs in the living room; these are placed around a coffee table, facing a small adobe fireplace. All other furnishings are modest and sparse. The walls are painted warm, rust ochre and three large, iron-barred windows look out onto a shared courtyard. (Carly tells us later that clothes are often dried on the window's iron bars with socks on each protuberance.) A beautiful red flowering tree is the focal point of the courtyard. The only sign of a television comes from a small side room into which the boys frequently disappear ... and then reappear.

An interesting and odd (to us) observation: As hard-pressed as they are for money, the family still hires a housekeeper. (This was the norm when Carly lived with families in Chile and Argentina as well.) What we think of as middle- to lower-class households commonly employ those on a lower rung of the social ladder to do their mundane household chores such as dusting, mopping, toilets, laundry and ironing. I can't imagine the pittance these housekeepers must earn. I asked Carly what this was like: "I always tried to say hello to her," Carly begins (the housekeeper being an indigenous woman with long braided hair, wearing a traditional long skirt), "but she seemed very shy and intimidated by me. My bottles of toiletries and my shoes were always placed in a neat line while I was gone. I imagine my laundry was done by her too." Rosa had recently fired a teenage Quichua girl and replaced her with this more mature indigenous woman.

An Inauspicious Start

It takes a little longer than anticipated for Courtney and me to leave for the day's venture. After busily preparing our daypacks in the privacy of our (their) bedroom, I seize the doorknob to exit, as I am wont to do, and the whole apparatus falls off right into my hand! Taken by surprise, I hold it up for view in a shaft of sunlight. "Oh noooooooo! **We broke their door!**" and furthermore, "**We're totally locked in**!" I desperately try to put it back and fix it while Courtney anxiously hovers over me, making me sweat. Inevitably, we have to start yelling for help. Javier comes to our rescue and from the other side of the door explains it is an ongoing problem. With the turn of a screwdriver he sets his gringa-people free. Ugh!

So then ... less than four steps out the door, still in the courtyard, Courtney is immediately nipped by one of the compounds nastier dogs. **"MOM!"** Great. Not twenty-four hours in the country and this has to happen. Wide-eyed Courtney looks at me with trepidation as we examine her leg. No skin is broken and most of the impact was absorbed by her pant leg. I make the parental decision to go on with our day, rejecting the good doctor's advice to seek emergency medical attention. And I hope I'm right.

Stepping out of the gated compound, we are finally on our own. I can't believe I'm actually in South America again! My poor brain is still in the surreal state of suspension brought on by jet travel, trying to catch up with my body and straining to make cognitive sense out of all the new, fast-incoming stimuli (i.e., I'm spacey).

Under a muted sky, on a battered cobblestone street, the white-washed neighborhood is mostly deserted this early afternoon, save the stray, straggly dog. The lane, more like an alleyway, is all about stone and cement and cinder blocks and fenced enclosures—with smatterings of potted flowers visible through unintentional fissures that reveal private courtyards. The residences are of a modest to impoverished nature with an occasional opulent home thrown in. Curious. All of them display a careful attention to security (as we are to find everywhere in Ecuador) of locked terraces, razor wire, and colorful glass shards atop high fences (the glass somewhat pretty, actually, when glowing in the sunlight). Even a preschool we pass,

Jardín Infantil, exhibits a glass shard embedded window treatment amidst cheerily painted-on pooh bears. Strange.

Locked out and looking from the outside, there's not much activity overall; it is seemingly lifeless. Unfortunately, Courtney and I stand out like the conspicuous foreigners we are. It is an uneasy feeling, but what is our recourse? Dress like natives? Dye our hair black? There really seems no way around looking like awkward tourists. (Carly: "You can't. Just give it up.")

We pass a large graffitied wall (which later comes to serve as a landmark for our particular neighborhood) that reads:

¿Quién es el terrorista? ¿Estados Unidos o Afganistán?
(Who is the terrorist? The United States or Afghanistan?)

With Courtney-translated directions from Rosa (I always just nod my head and pretend to understand when spoken to in rapid Spanish) we attempt to make our way to Otavalo's famous downtown market: walk several blocks *norte*, turn right at the *dinosaurios* (*Dinosaurs, what? Are you sure you translated right Courtney?*)* left on *Calle Sucre* and head two more kilometers into town. No, it doesn't take long at all before Courtney and I are lost and bickering amongst ourselves. (I say left at a main junction and she says right as we vainly try to recall the route of our one a.m. entrance into town the night before.) At this junction and despite Courtney's mortifying protest (sending her fleeing down the street in the opposite direction of humiliating parent) I seek out two young men I spot lingering on a highly trafficked street corner. They both look a bit indisposed at my approach. I humbly ask for directions. In strained English, the collegiate-looking (neat backpack, jeans, baseball cap) *Otavaleño* obliged my request. At the end of his directions, he takes my hand in both of his and so kindheartedly says, "I am so happy to help you." Wow, I wasn't expecting that. (*Humph!* Courtney.)

From the extreme quiet of the neighborhood, it does not take long to get into a calamitous parade of crazed traffic whizzing past us at a

---

* She did. Though the topiary display on the medium strip was a little beaten down and hard to distinguish, it did produce an *Aha!* moment of Brontosaurus recognition.

breakneck speed. We must take great care upon crossing these main thoroughfares and are twice separated, with me stranded on a grassy meridian. Courtney makes it across without me and shoots me a look of concern/annoyance above all the car roofs. Standing in the middle of the four-lane miasma, I make a somewhat pained attempt to look nonchalant and natural while waiting for the infinitely long traffic light to change, all the while inhaling copious amounts of exhaust fumes. Nothing like awkwardly standing out.

Eventually, and purely by happenstance, we close in on Otavalo's city-center marketplace.

My visual summarization of Otavalo that last day in July:
(pronounced *oh tah vah low* by the way—no accent on any syllable)

The city is cradled within alluring mountainous peaks buffeted by stormy clouds—peaks not so tall as to be awe-inspiring, but high enough to beckon the adventurous with its precipices and hidden crannies. The area, though ruggedly stunning, appears strained by a harshness wrought by the wind and sun (high altitude-low latitude syndrome), the paucity of lush trees or robust vegetation a reflection of the weather's severity.' While Courtney and I walk the outskirts, our high noon perspective is not very appealing; asphalt bleak comes to mind (but that also describes my hometown on its outskirts and busy thoroughfares). Perhaps at another time of day or year things look a bit more flourishing; there is a rainy and dry season.

The slopes of the surrounding hills are replete with agricultural fields and along the horizon there is a sporadic plume from smoking fires. The hilltop fires are alarming to see at first, but it is later explained that the farmers here still practice slash and burn agriculture.

Within the larger Province of *Imbabura,* the city of Otavalo began (perhaps as long as 4,000 years ago) as a crossroads, a meeting and trading

---

* Never did I imagine that upon returning home to Yakima (an irrigated desert-like, sage land) I would be overwhelmed by the apparition of lush trees and vegetation: In comparison to highland Ecuador it all looked so incredibly thriving, bursting with health and water-rich vitality.

center for the wider farming community. Over time, the city center has been transformed into a world-renowned market due to the skill and industriousness of its resident and surrounding native populations—about 70,000 souls. (Over half of the city's population consists of indigenous peoples.) Specifically held in high regard are their superb textiles and weavings. The market is the oldest and best-known in all South America, and we are eager to see it.

After reading all the introductory literature about the market's famed status, I am somewhat expecting a town of relative, cohesive charm, but instead my senses are flooded with a dissonant hodgepodge of building styles, all tinged with a weather-worn patina. Corrugated tin roofs cover flaking plaster walls; heavily mortared cinder blocks rest against primitive mud brick; sticks and grasses protrude, even grow, from dilapidated rooftops; rust-colored tile on adobe and red brick structures charm; Spanish colonial cathedrals stand adjacent to seventies-style, vacant-looking office buildings; and masses of tangled electrical wires hang betwixt skilled displays of public art. The city is not cosmetically refined by any means, but it's still fascinating.

After a self-directed tour of *disorientation*, Courtney and I finally meet up with an exuberant Carly for a late lunch. She's exuberant because *her vacation* begins with us too and she has worked very hard these past few weeks. I always marvel at Carly in these foreign environments. She never seems more alive, glowing with competence and self-assured energy, completely in her element.* She knows exactly where to go: a cozy café popular with her volunteer crowd that serves amazing fresh bread sandwiches, smoothies (*batidos*), and *real* coffee (this is huge).

We are greeted by a young, lovely Afro-Ecuadorian woman who kindly seats us to take our order. I notice the ceiling is concealed by a unique treatment of crisscrossed wooden slats hanging down by chains; the warm wood tones have the effect of softening the ubiquitous, harsh, fluorescent lighting prevalent in most buildings. Upbeat music that I find very appealing is playing on the café's sound system. Carly identifies it

---

* Although, it is necessary to knock her down a peg or two when she gets too cocky.

45

as a popular style called *Reggaetón.*[*] I have no idea what they're singing about (in Spanish), but I like it. The delightful, small café of mismatched wood tables and bamboo-trimmed walls is packed with customers. The delicious food is unbelievably cheap; it's a little over two dollars each for plenty of quality, fresh food. (We had blackberry *batidos*, avocado and cheese sandwiches made from a fresh loaf of bread, and precious *real* coffee.)

Heading out, Carly is thrilled to show us around. The cultural experience is, as usual, an onslaught to the senses. Walking down the congested streets, within all the bustling, jostling traffic of humanity and automobiles, one of the startling images to immediately catch my eye is the dress of some indigenous women: their heads are swathed in heavy black fabric and they are wearing ankle-length black or dark indigo skirts. The overall effect (fright) is that of an austere religious order of nuns.[†] (This stark black is in high contrast to the Quechuas' rainbow rush of color I experienced on a trip to Cuzco, Peru, though I suspect much of that display was for the sake of tourism.) In due time, I notice this subdued manner of dress is often accessorized with indigo, maroon or fuchsia fabrics, such as a shawl or *manta* (carrying cloth on the back) and usually features a beautifully embroidered white blouse underneath. A distinctive adornment for many of the female *indígena* Otavaleñas are the multiple upon multiple layers of gold beads draped around the neck as well as their red coral bracelets.

All manner of bizarre sights greet my gaze as we navigate through the rush of people. Again, we have to be very cognizant of our surroundings at all times due to the high traffic. Frequently, Carly's arm unexpectedly *thrusts out* and presses me back, alerting me to stop carefully and patiently at every intersection. Glancing into an open-door *farmacia* (pharmacy) I see there is a deep, gaping hole dug out of the tile floor. High dirt mounds are piled along the sides, yet the patrons simply navigate around them while going about their business. (Suing must not be a national pastime. In the USA,

---

* "Reggaetón's origin represents a hybrid of many different musical genres and influences from various countries in the Caribbean, Latin America and the United States."[2]

† Fright for me because I am a recovering Catholic, slapped around by nuns from the dark ages. (All right, I was no saint either—I *probably* deserved some of it … but not all of it!) Those hellacious hacks I received (bent over)—by a mad nun wielding a three foot board with drilled-out *speed* holes—produced some real nerve-tingling *pain!*)

citizens are more apt to fling themselves into the hole and claim a lifelong disability). I brush past armed guards standing stoically outside bank doors and get a close-up view of their holstered firearms. Looking up over the chaotic traffic there are very young children sitting, *teetering* on the back gate of pick-up trucks, moving along right in the middle of the city's busy streets; one bump and they'd be on the pavement and underneath the next closely following vehicle! Helmet-free motorcyclists whiz around it all with one to three exposed kids clinging to their backs. And there are, as usual, so many poor, neglected dogs scavenging for food everywhere. Within all this chaos of pedestrians, errant dogs, motorcycles, trucks, and cars, it does not take long before we are truly mystified as to why there is not a daily fatality. ("There should be dead bodies on every street!" declares Carly!)

Any semblance of dignity or iota of sanity
Swept Away By Market Madness

From the exterior, the famous Otavalo market looks slightly underwhelming, even dreary. It consists of about an acre of canopy-covered marketers within a palm-treed town square. Initially unimpressed, I enter the aisles with the girls and nonchalantly saunter among the stalls. I begin perusing the goods, impervious and resolute to any kind of self-indulgence, thinking I have clearly evolved beyond the base human desire of materialism.

In a stealth-like manner, intense color sensations start to seep into my brain ... like the drip, drip, drip of an intoxicatingly, sweet nectar. Moving along from one SUPER DOSE OF VIBRANT COLOR to the next stall's SUPER DOSE OF VIBRANT COLOR my resolve begins to weaken. There are mountains of indigenous items for barter that are glorious, skillfully hand-crafted and exactly the kind of things I like—scarves! hammocks! blankets! hats! bracelets! bags! Every color receptor in my brain is flooded and over-stimulated. My self-programmed override is blinking an emergency warning: You do not need more *things*, remember you are spiritually evolved. Step away from the stalls! Step away from the stalls!

BUT THIS STUFF IS REALLY BEAUTIFUL, THE KIND OF STUFF I REALLY LIKE and furthermore the prices are REALLY low!!!

Just one modest little purchase won't hurt ...

And that's how it all began.

Blissed-out on color is the best way I can describe my shopping mania. Delirious, cuckoo for coca' puffs, however you want to put it, I am clearly out of control. I find gifts for everybody I know and matching ones for myself. Before long, Carly takes me aside and calmly reassures, "Mother, we will be here for *three days*. Take a break. I want to show you one of my favorite *batido* hang-out spots." Just across the street, she leads us up some

---

* The Incas introduced coca leaf chewing (coca being the source of cocaine) to the local inhabitants when they conquered the area in the 1400s.

stairs to a Mexican restaurant featuring an outdoor deck overlooking the market. She thinks I'm going to rest for a while, soak in the ambiance.

The three of us are lucky to find a free table among the six offered outside and we quickly claim one of worn wood with a yellow market umbrella flapping, nay spinning, in the wind. We plunk ourselves and our treasures down to boldly face one another. The girls have never seen me like this before—so overcome with shopping fever—and are somewhat aghast at my newly-revealed weakness of character. (Though I think Courtney, with a perceptible smirk, is slightly entertained.) They are shopping as well, but the rules are different for their materialism-decrying Mama. *But this is different!* I rationalize.

Compounding my insanity, I decide it's time to really let loose and order a round of caffeinated Coca-Colas®. We normally don't indulge in pop so this is a major departure for us. We all get one and partake of a product of extraordinary popularity here in Latin America. I don't understand the overwhelming pervasiveness of Coke—the drink is *everywhere*, even added to beer! (I strongly suspect that the coca leaf ingredient has not been completely neutralized, but I can't prove it.) ' South of our border, Cokes always seem to have an extra *dazzling* sparkle; I know the original cane sugar is replaced with corn syrup in the U.S. beverage, but what a noticeable difference!

Between the Cokes and the shopping fever, it's not long before I'm feeling antsy again. (Think Scarlett O'Hara's darting eyes while concocting a scheme.) Somehow, I have to ditch the girls and their judgmental stares.

"Uh, I have to go to the bathroom … I'll be right back," I announce.

I run down the stairs and out the door. Before either can say, "Where's Mom," they spot me once again among the merchant stalls below. I can feel

---

*   Once, a few years back, for a treat during the Christmas holidays, I decided to indulge in Coca-Cola®. As the girls observed with astonishment, I quickly became addicted ("COKE!"), leaving them in running vehicles while pursuing fixes from beautiful, glowing, roadside vending machines. (How could I have not noticed these before!) I am convinced there's a secret, addictive quality to this beverage. Did you know the Coca-Cola ® Corporation is one of only a handful of companies that can legally import coca leaves (for *flavoring*) to the U.S.?

their burning gaze, their *tsk tsks*, as I look up to return a feeble wave. They watch as a (mis)match of wits plays out: A savvy *indígena* businesswoman has me locked in her sights (the locals are known for their well-honed ability to effectively size up customers). I retreat several times to resist the lapis lazuli earrings that so tempt me. With each backward step, she is determined not to let me get away and skillfully reels me back in. By the fourth price reduction I finally succumb. I certainly don't want to insult her and the integrity of her jewelry!

Purchase in hand, ashamed at how low I've sunk and how quickly, I skulk back to the girls, still sitting at the restaurant, still waiting to share some quality face time with their mother. Remorse fills me. "I shouldn't have bought these," I lament. And then a light bulb idea occurs to me, "Maybe I can take them back!"

"MOTHER YOU CANNOT RETURN ITEMS TO THE INDIGENOUS PEOPLE!" Carly sneers, interjecting some much-needed common sense. "We are moving on!"

From this tourist mecca, we head for a more authentic flavor that caters to the local population: the open-air food market. But first, we must pass through a street bazaar serving the quotidian needs of the locals. It is a mishmash of goods for sale amid the loud cacophony of music: speakers blare Reggaetón and Rap from CD stores; there are rows of blue jeans, posters, toiletry items, brooms and cleaning products; rows and rows of shoes; and lots of knock-off brand clothing, such as Nike and Adidas sportswear. Nothing we would be interested in purchasing, but still interesting. Everywhere we go we have to jockey for walking space on the hot, bland asphalt amid hordes of shoppers.

Once we turn the corner into the food market we are hit with another blast of color, but this time of an agrarian kind. Piles and piles of vibrant fruits and vegetables, varieties as such I have never seen before, line both sides of the street. Ecuador produces around fifty varieties of potatoes and bananas, and several strange specimens are on display—like short, fat, red bananas and purple-black, finger potatoes. Wow, this is great! The market is bustling with commerce; stalls and stalls of colorful produce are artfully displayed and bursting with field-fresh vitality. Given that this is where Carly shopped weekly for her school duties, we soon come upon a produce merchant that she has befriended. *Corina*, a twentyish mestizo woman, greets Carly in a flourish of hugs, smiles and rapid-Spanish endearments. Surveying Corina's produce stand, Carly is anxious for us to try a small, red, prickly-looking fruit called an *achotillo*. The *achotillo* (also known as rambutan) is a fruit originating from the warm tropical climates of Indonesia, now grown in countries that are within 15 degrees of the equator. Exterior peeled, the grape-sized edible portion inside is sour-sweet and its whitish, pink flesh is only sucked rather than swallowed. We all take a sample. "It is good!" we agree in smiles! Though we try several times, Corina adamantly refuses to let us pay for the fruit; she wants to give the treat to Carly and her American family as a farewell gift. We are all touched by her generosity, knowing life can be such a struggle here. There's a tinge of sadness as Carly and Corina take an embracing, farewell picture together, knowing it is most likely the two will never see one other again.

Ambling away from Corina's stall by myself, I come upon a postcard photo waiting to happen: Leaning against a lamppost is an antiquated, burnt-orange bicycle modified to push a vivid blue, old wood, wagon bed—the owner is nowhere to be found. Its makeshift bed overflows with all manner of colorful produce. I look around to notice numerous bicyclers carrying their bounty to market in this manner. The scene is so picturesque and so utterly foreign.

Our First Hotel

We had arranged to stay for only one night with Rosa and Javier, so it was time to move on to our hotel accommodations. It is mid afternoon when Carly leads us to the city's central district. From what we had experienced before in Latin American lodgings, amid the loud cacophony of street life, one has only to find the Alice in Wonderland passageway, the gate that reveals the door to a secret world. *Ahhhhhh*, we arrive at the oasis: The Doña Esther Hotel.

Beneath a tasteful, hand-carved sign, easy to miss among the blitz of cheap commercial signage, we find a large, locked wrought iron gate. Peering behind the gate we see a small, charming garden and seating bench. We cannot, however, gain access to this alternate world without first providing a secret password. For us this means pressing the intercom, identifying our reservation-holding selves and presto! we are admitted. First meandering down a cool, dark hallway, we pass by a reading room and fireplace to our left. Nice. However, the pièce de résistance emerges with the open sky, central courtyard. Enclosed on all sides by four levels of hotel rooms (only twelve rooms in all) is a quaint Shangri-La, a sanctuary of peace and serenity: burbling fountain, water-dripping flora, decorative art tile on walls and tumbled stone designs underfoot. One would never know the chaos that exists just outside this heavenly insulated space. Oversized wood doors on one side of the courtyard open into the hotel restaurant, revealing a large, impressive, burnt sienna, clay oven. Tables are provided in the courtyard for outdoor dining as well. Though nothing is ritzy chic, it's just perfect for us.

We move across the plaza to the reservation desk, a dark and tiny room off the hallway. Carly had secured "The Penthouse" on the rooftop floor. At $45 a night, it is the hotel's honeymoon suite and the only room with a fireplace. And I love fireplaces! After placing our passports and anything else of value (not much) in the hotel safe, we lug our backpacked selves up the four flights of stairs. The teal blue handrail aesthetically matches the railings that line each landing, complementing the golden-wood doors of the hotel rooms. Before long it is a dizzying look down at the sequestered square, all adorned with hanging plants and climbing bougainvillea.

Once at the top, we must circumvent a German tourist lazily occupying a hammock strung along the open, covered walkway. He is taking in the blissful panorama of the city, all the way to the mountain tops. ' Though the rooftop consists mostly of bleak, gray cement, there is a colorful array of guest laundry strung along a clothesline just beyond our hotel door. It is wonderful. We were issued a huge black skeleton key—the likes of which Captain Hook would use—to open the hand-carved, double, wood doors to our Penthouse.

---

* This guy really tried to hog that hotel-issued hammock. After two days of his relentless occupancy I couldn't take it anymore. Fortunately, I had thought to bring along some wind-up predatory arachnids I'd wisely bought in the Yucatan. Boy did he jump. (I love hammocks and the view *really was* great.)

A Fireplace of My Own

"... fires have strange and wonderful powers. Even their memories make life the adventure it was meant to be." Sigurd F. Olson

For our first evening in the hotel, Carly had agreed to meet her former colleagues for a farewell dinner and drink. Courtney decides to go along for a taste of the nightlife here in Otavalo. I am left for an evening alone in my new environment. I carefully note the physical characteristics of my Penthouse suite (in case I decide to write about it later). The three separate rooms have an agreeable, fresh air atmosphere due to large windows and an unobstructed rooftop view over the city. The most striking feature is the exposed timber beams that cross the ceiling of the main sitting area as well as in the large adjoining bedroom; the bedroom possesses large, room darkening shutters. The floor is painted a burnt orange in stark contrast to the pale lime green adobe walls. There's blackened soot above the well-used fireplace and a singular gold, plastic light fixture hangs down over the center of a table. Though things appear a bit worn, the artisan touches of the carved, double-entry door, clever window shutters (besides the normal opening, they are halved midway down, allowing endless light and air options), and large chestnut armoire in the bedroom make for charming accommodations. We even have a small kitchen with its own small, window view. I love it.

As night descends in this High Andes altitude the temperature dips, the air is chilled, and a fire is most welcome. Candles have been provided for the fireplace mantle, one a natural clay holder appropriately in the shape of an iguana. Upon lighting the tall, slender white candles, I cannot believe the metamorphosis that takes place within this room. As if by magic, the candlelit adobe walls at once become redolent with warmth, character and mystery. Outside the picture window the view glows with the blue and gold of a nearby colonial church; its rounded dome and twin steeples light up the hillside. In the darkness below I can hear the traffic, men whistling, and music drifting up from stereos. The glaring daylight has shifted to the strange vagaries of street nightlife. I'm thinking, *If I were a brilliant writer down on my luck, this place exudes the perfect atmosphere for the toiling, solitary artist.**

Once I get the adobe fireplace lit (not easy), I lie next to it, listen to the street sounds and relish this most sublime experience.

---

*   I tried hard to feel down on my luck ... but no brilliant musings poured forth.

You Don't Know What You've Got Till It's Gone

Very first thing, next morning after my shower, I plug in my carefully thought out, small travel hair dryer to instantly hear *sssssssssssph pffffftt* accompanied by black incinerating smoke. No more hair dryer. Great. That's $25 quite literally gone up in smoke. This is typical, even with an adaptor/converter, for American products to *destroy or be destroyed* by foreign systems.* I am thereafter held captive to the strange proclivities of my hair's innate, steely determination to dip, flip and protrude sideways.

However, the fact that our room provides hot, dependable, showers is a huge plus! At first, the significance is lost on Courtney and me: Reading the hotel's advertising brochure we had been puzzled by their marked promotion of "Hot Showers." Huh? What's the big deal? That's to be expected isn't it? No, *it is a big deal*.

Carly, on the other hand, thoroughly grasps this precious commodity. Painfully denied a hot bath for weeks, she completely gives herself over to the blissful decadence of plentiful, luxurious, warm water! Engulfing the bathroom with hot roiling steam, pouring forth like storm clouds into the sitting room, she ecstatically proclaims from the shower how *we have no idea* what it's like to be without, how hot water is such a vastly under-appreciated pleasure that we take for granted! (Just set your next ten baths on "ice cold": instant appreciation!) Most people in the world do not have such easy, plentiful access.

Once we're all bathed, brushed, lips moisturized, fresh make-up applied, we emerge prepared—just as all intrepid explorers who have gone before us—to tackle our first day roaming the environs of Otavalo.

---

*   We have shorted-out foreign hotels before, soon accompanied by a miffed hotel manager knocking at our door, muttering his hatred for energy-zapping, American-bought products on steroids.

55

August One

The Bus Ride

Determined to take part in the local culture as much as possible, Carly insists we take the *public* bus up to our hiking destination (or at least as far as the bus goes) to a mountainous region above the city. First, we walk at least two miserable miles along the horrifically busy main highway just to get to the bus interchange. We stop at an all-cement, multi-intersecting junction of whizzing congestion to await our bus, confused and hoping we are in the right spot. A million buses go by until we (Carly) are able to recognize the correct signage on the bus. Handing over our 25 cent fee, we three, pack-bearing gringas, step up and turn to face a sea of *indígena* faces … and no open seats. Okay, *I really want to stick out even more by standing up*, but there is no alternative. Carly and I manage to stay together, but Courtney's place behind me is superseded by an aggressive duo and she is trapped right behind the bus driver a few bodies down from us.

The bus kicks into gear. Hang on! Here we go.

Grasping tightly onto the overhead bar, with each jolt of the bus I list into the laps of the couple seated beneath me. And it's made far worse when someone needs to push down the aisle behind me. I try to apologize, *"¡Perdón! ¡Perdón!"* each time I intrusively lurch into their personal space. But the middle-aged man and woman remain strangely tranquil; they seem used to the status quo (though maybe not by a pale-white interloper like me) and graciously yield their lap space whenever needed. *"¡No hay problema! Está bien!"* I hear.

As we're jostling up the hillside on the winding two-lane road, I try to glance over to see how Courtney's doing, but can only catch the back of her bobbing, strawberry-blond head amongst all the intervening, dark-headed bodies. Though we are thoroughly jam-packed NO NEW CUSTOMERS ARE EVER TURNED AWAY! At each stop a bus employee, hanging on an exterior bar outside the open door (and presumably trained in a sardine factory) jumps to the ground and literally yanks people off the bus (to stay on schedule I suppose) while physically *pushing* the newcomers on and in. I can't believe it. With each new body we all have to try to contract our physical selves to smaller and smaller entities (who needs oxygen) as I get more and more up-close and personal with my seated new acquaintances. (*So what do you two think about my new bra and ample American bosoms?* I could have easily asked them.)

With each incoming passenger making their way down the aisle behind me, I begin to wonder if I am inadvertently cheating on my marriage vows; the pushing and prodding is a very intimate experience.

After about five miles, we are ejected (and I mean ejected) at the tail end of the bus route where it will loop around and head back down the hill. Adios crazy bus! However, we still have some distance to go to get to our hiking destination and it is now necessary to flag down a ride. This is quite customary and it does not take long before we are able to hail a vehicle. One problem though, it is a pick-up truck offering a ride in the back of the open bed. We need to discuss the ensuing dilemma of safety or fun, while the truck driver idles, impatiently awaiting our decision. We retreat to the back of the truck, huddled in discussion. Courtney balks and votes "**NO!**" at the dangerous open-air prospect and Carly votes "**YES!**" and both turn their gaze to me in search of some motherly wisdom, or at least to cast the tie-breaker decision. "Hell yes," votes mom. So confident I would side with safety, Courtney's mouth drops open in bare-faced shock. "Why not?" I say. "It could be fun!" Soon the three of us are seated in the open flatbed, mom in the middle, backs against the cab, careening up the hillside. Fortunately, it is great fun. We get to see the countryside without the filter of a smudged window, and the mountain air is exhilarating.

As we're climbing the hillside we pass several rural homesteads, rambling and self-made mud brick dwellings. We see *indígenas* tending their fields, hanging laundry, and feeding chickens, pigs and goats. I view with curiosity one lone "dude" (he looks like a Westernized rapper, thirtyish, buff, sunglasses and goatee) setting up giant outdoor stereo speakers on a platform outside his hut. *Hmmmm?*

Reaching the trailhead in a couple of miles, we disembark, tip the driver, and take off, up and through some tall brush on a well-marked pathway. Quickly emerging into an open landscape of scant vegetation we are hit with a stunning, eye-straining, aqua blue lake to our left, and the city of

Otavalo spread out far below to the right. *Laguna Cuicocha* or Cuicocha Lake, lies in the crater of an extinct volcano that last erupted some 3000 years ago. The protruding dome makes a double island in the middle of the lake. I read in our guide that natives come to this area during the summer solstice to make offerings.

Everywhere is deserted except for the occasional motor boat droning far below toward the island. We are bedecked in hats and drenched in sunscreen; the sun is harsh and the air is thin. We traipse a couple of strenuous, panting miles up the 8 km. crater-encircling pathway only to have it dawn on us, *Hey, we can do this at home.* Though spectacular, we are used to such high mountain scenery due to our proximity to several dormant volcanoes in Washington State and decide our energies would be best spent pursuing sights of a more foreign nature. We are all in agreement at this juncture to reverse course and head back down and across the valley to *Parque Cóndor*, a wildlife refuge featuring the renowned (and endangered) Andean Condor among several other raptors.

Sitting in dirt like vagrants on the roadside, we must now wait for a taxi. Carly attempts to hail a ride, sticking her arm out at every passing vehicle. Several cars zoom by with a shake of the head. Finally, after about a 25-minute wait, we are lucky to snag a taxi. Weary of multiple transports, we spend the extra money and ask to be taken straight to the Condor Park, completely on the other side of the valley and up the opposing mountainside. Zoom! Here we go again, glad for the open window breeze and to be comfortably sitting once again.

As the Spanish speaker, Carly is always in the front seat, making conversation. This nearly always proves to be enriching, since the locals often open up to Carly's fluency, especially when she identifies herself as a teacher working in the province (teachers are held in high esteem). The spark ignites and the mestizo man begins eagerly pointing out areas of interest, proud of his homeland. After rushing across the valley floor, the ascending mountain road changes to a single lane of rough cobblestone (i.e., the ride gets *very, very bumpy*). After passing through some tiny, chicken-squawking, laundry-hanging settlements (no matter how small, there's always a church, *fascinating*) we break into soft, blowing grasses amid gorgeous green hillsides. The road stretches up and up the steep hillside, zigzagging through some of the most exquisite scenery I've yet encountered. Open tilled fields of greenery wave under a blustery, strong sky. Our driver tells us the acres of tilled landscape—maize, quinoa, potatoes, as far as the eye can see—are still entirely cultivated by hand, oxen and plow.

Out of enthusiasm and pride our driver decides to take us on a detour via a significantly rougher and unpaved road in order to show us a special tree, one that is sacred and steeped in magical lore. Anticipating a spectacle of some grandeur, fit for reverence and justifying all this road dust effort, we eventually come upon one lone stubby tree in a scraggy vacant field, visually quite underwhelming. *Hmmmm*, what to make of this? The significance and potency lost on our transitory tourist brains. Apparently, this tree known as *El Lechero* (The Milk) is believed to have healing powers worthy of a continuous pilgrimage by locals. Perhaps if we had had more time and depth of insight we could have been more appreciative of this brief encounter ... through a car window ... darkly. But, *que sé yo?* (What do I know?)

Driving on to the nature conservancy, I am very excited to see a *Cóndor Andina* (Andean Condor) in its native land. I had read so much over the years about their mythological significance to native cultures as symbols of spiritual power. The girls are not as psyched as I am, rather just indulging mom, but once we're dropped off and walk through the entry gate of this impressive, smartly designed park, their enthusiasm quickly rises. We follow winding, stone-paved pathways among spacious, outdoor, caged enclosures harboring a menagerie of strange raptors and birds of prey like owls, falcons, eagles, vultures, and hawks. We stop dead in our tracks at our first sight of a Harpy Eagle—this hefty bird weighs twenty pounds and has a wingspan of six feet. To my untrained eyes it looks something like a cross between a monkey and an owl; its feathers, in alarm mode at our presence, are sticking straight-up out of its primate-like head. Very eerie looking. I found the origin of its name "Harpy" to be quite interesting.

> Its name refers to the harpies of Ancient Greek mythology. These were wind spirits that took the dead to Hades, and were said to have a body like an eagle and the face of a human. Their curved talons are up to five inches (12.5 cm) long, as long as the claws of a grizzly bear. It is the

59

largest and most powerful raptor found in America, and among the largest extant species of eagles in the world. It usually inhabits tropical lowland rainforests in the upper (emergent) canopy layer.[3]

I see now where creators of bizarre face masks get inspiration! Courtney, who approached the thought of visiting a bird sanctuary with ill-concealed disdain, excitedly snaps photo after photo. I am glad they both seem to be enjoying the experience after all. (Of course I point out my innate superiority—repeatedly—for having suggested the excursion in the first place.)

Finally, coming upon the tethered Condor, my breath is taken away at the immensity of this bird. Simply *reading* the statistics that they are four-foot high with a ten-foot wingspan is just not the same as standing next to one. Wow. This is a very intimidating vulture. It is slightly repulsive *knowing why* their head and neck are featherless (bald): for hygienic reasons this feature provides a cleaner entrance and exit out of a scavenged carcass as well as facilitating sterilization by high altitude sun radiation. *Ewwwwwwww.* It is the largest bird of prey in the world and known to soar as high as 18,000 feet. Distinctively, the *Cóndor Andinas* has a white downy collar at the base of the neck just to keep warm in the Andes.

> The birds are a source of national pride across South America and play a prominent role in folklore and cultural mythology. They have been represented in Andean art since 2500 BC. The Incas believed the condor brought the sun into the sky every morning and was a messenger to the gods.[4]

Rounding the last corner of the reserve we come upon some happy-faced people exiting from a stunning mountain-edge amphitheater. They are all ecstatic because they had just witnessed a spectacular falconry show (apparently one falcon took off into the wild blue yonder, never to return). *Nooooooooo!* We are too late and the next show is not for another three hours! I listen to exaltations floating above the wowed crowd like "Awesome," "Breathtaking" and "Amazing." This makes me crabby; I become harpy-faced. *"Do you really want to wait three hours for the next show,"* asks an exasperated Carly, "'cause we can wait for three more hours for the next show if you reeeeeeeally want to!"

No, but this will be added to my growing list of frustrating near misses.

Growing List of Frustrating Near Misses

2004: March, France. My one and only trip to Paris. We arrive wiped-out, jet lagged, and exhausted from carrying our over-packed, family-of-four luggage (Mark, me, Carly, Courtney) in elevator-less, economy hotel up three flights of tiny, winding, wrought iron stairs. Young adult daughters have strength to leave at night while old parents pass out. I completely miss the **Eiffel Tower all ablaze in lights.** (Though, before leaving us, our jet lagged, wide-eyed and non-blinking Courtney proclaims, "I have no thoughts in my head.")

2005: June, Cuzco, Peru. While there we learn Cuzco puts on a spectacular, world-renowned **Summer Solstice reenactment of Incan Rituals**. We just happen to be there the week before.

2008: November, New York, NY. Time constraints have us leaving *the day before* the **Rockefeller Christmas Tree** is lit. (My niece Kristy, who we were visiting, cruelly e-mails later as to how truly wondrous it is to see in person!)

2008: April, Yucatan Peninsula. A highly-recommended night music and **laser show** produced on the ancient pyramids of the **Uxmal Mayan Ruins**. Carly and I (the travelers) were really looking forward to it. The pre-planned travel itinerary we signed up for did not mention they were in the middle of renovations and thus the show was temporarily canceled. I spent the entire evening sitting, soaking and sulking in a hotel pool *just outside* the closed entry gate, thinking about what could have been. (I did enjoy the swim, a Cheshire moon and stunningly clear stars.)

2009: August, this trip: **Riobamba open-air train ride through the Andes Mountains**. The ride through *Nariz Del Diablo* (Nose of the Devil) is listed among the top ten of most desirable world adventures. We miss it (explanation later).

Dorothy E. Groszhans

2010: June, Barcelona, Spain. The historical **Sardana dance**: spontaneous dance derived from a native Catalan tradition in a political show of unity. Out for the Sunday evening *paseo* (walk), people randomly join in circles, throw down purses and valuables in the center, lock arms and follow intricate dance steps, accompanied by live street music. This takes place *every Sunday* on the Las Ramblas Plaza, exactly where Kristy, Carly, Courtney and I are staying. We are leaving for Cadaques … on *Saturday*.

Otavalo at Night

Just like cities everywhere, Otavalo teenagers cruise the city's central square in hopped-up cars, their music pounding and blaring from car speakers. We decide to leave the city center this evening, and head up a steep, lantern-lit staircase that winds up to the top of a hillside. Following the stone steps we soon encounter children playing on a landing beneath the streetlight— lanes of adobe dwellings are nearby. Carly extends a *"buenas tardes"* (good afternoon) to a group of adorable little girls who emphatically respond in chorus, "¡**ES BUENAS NOCHES**!" (**It's good NIGHT!**) *Well, thank you for the correction!* At the top of the flight we find ourselves high above the city in a dark, alien world. Railroad tracks run beside an unbroken wall of adobe residences, their doors and windows shaded and locked. Only one man with a toddler are out walking the tracks together.* The toddler extends a very sweet *"buenas noches"* to us. We return the greeting and then pause on a viewpoint, and try to absorb the beauty of Otavalo's twinkling, golden city lights spread far below.

On our descent we are sure to issue a hearty *buenas noches* this time to the same trio of little girls. They respond in like, not bothering to look up from their game. Near the bottom of the stairs, in what seems an industrial, paved parking lot, a volleyball game is in progress; it is so dimly lit there's barely enough light to see anything.

We head to a café right on the market plaza. The tiny, dark wood, restaurant is like any we would find in the U.S.; however, the scene outside is anything but. We are perched on high café chairs over a miniscule table, right in front of the window, drinking *batidos* through straws and watching the marketers pack up for the evening. I have never seen anything like this before: All the merchandise is bundled into a white tarp, humongous square cube— say six by six foot—to which a strap is attached. The venders, men and women, place the strap across their forehead, hoist the giant cube on their back, lean forward at a severe angle and transport their heavy goods away. Astounding! I see that some are taken to nearby lockers with rolling garage

---

*   For me railroad tracks, trains and their whistles at night always elicit a bittersweet feeling of loneliness, melancholy and the seductive mystery of travel. Perhaps the sound of the whistle is reminiscent of each life's solitary journey?

doors, secured right off the square; some are loaded onto awaiting trucks; and others disappear down the street with only the white, bobbing cube visible. I am in awe at how they carry these!

The sidewalks begin to light up with the harsh glaring light of sidewalk food vendors. Small, individual stands sizzle and fry various nighttime offerings like chicken, *cuy* (guinea pig), soups (tripe) and maize. The smell is heavy with smoke, cooking oil, and seared meat.

It's getting late and time to head back. Walking to our hotel, I spot an elderly Quichua woman within the shallow recess of a doorway; she is all huddled into a little ball, already sleeping in her bed for the night. It gets really cold here at night—the slight doorframe provides scant protection. *What can this be like?* I wonder. *Is she one of the market workers?*

A deep wave of sorrow sweeps through me.

Imagine A Latin American George Clooney …

Okay, more like the octogenarian George Burns, but still … I feel I need to record this.

Late one hot afternoon, the girls and I are traversing a deserted Otavalo street, save an elderly gentleman nicely dressed in a suit, sans tie, carrying a shopping bag. From his visage-buffering distance I can see that the man seems transfixed by something in my direction—as if by a vision. I glance over each shoulder to see where the girls are; but no, his hypnotic gaze is clearly centered on me. As he slowly makes his way toward me in a diagonal course across the cobblestone street, I have no idea what to expect. Is there a Virgin Mary stain on my t-shirt? A Jesus face smudged on my baseball cap? Gently taking my hand in his, and gazing at me as if I were The Madonna, a soft spoken Spanish fills the air.

"What is he saying Carly, what is he saying?" I plead, as my heavenly hands begin to perspire.

A bemused Carly translates: "Who is this lovely person? Is this your niece?"

Now that's simply ridiculous—but I'll take it. "Is this your cousin?" he persists.

His face registering (feigning) shocked disbelief at hearing, "*¡Ella es nuestra madre!*" ("She is our mother!" proclaims Carly.)

He continues to gaze longingly. I'm getting more and more uncomfortable. Geez, I'd have thought a close-up view would've broken the spell by now! I deduce he must have severe cataracts. As he continues to hold my hand I'm beginning to feel the fight or flight urge. (Good thing I didn't have my usual gallon canister of pepper spray with me.)

At last Carly breaks up the love fest and pronounces we need to move on. And I need to skitter away before I fall into some harsh lighting.

I would be remiss not mention our hotel's pleasurable, evening dining experiences. Our dinners are rich in organic comforts: candlelit tables welcome us in from the night chill and the modestly sized room is dominated by the flaming, burnt sienna clay oven. The walls are wainscoted in natural bamboo, the tables and chairs made of dark wood. On our second night we are serenaded by a four-piece Andean band. We listen to the sounds of a *churango* (guitar made from an armadillo shell), pan flute, drum and *güiro* (scraping gourd). The room's oversized mahogany doors are wide open to the courtyard where the all-male band is playing. Fire, clay, bamboo, and musical instruments that derive straight from the plant and animal kingdom infuse the ambience with visceral pleasure.

As is customary, evening diners are immediately served a small cylinder glass of unsolicited sugar cane liqueur. The *aguardiente* (burning water) is tasty but powerful! (With one sip I declare myself drunk—*I did feel it*— but neither girl believes me.) The drink is accompanied, strangely, by tiny servings of popcorn and baked corn kernels.

Seated nearby on our second night is a large table of ten German tourists in animated discussion, partaking of copious amounts of wines and beers— and placing all their dinner orders before ours. We know we have a very long wait after the three of us order our cheese avocado soup and bread. Later on, I see the soup is placed inside the clay oven and the resulting flavor proves exceptionally delicious (especially by the time it arrives).

Carly is the only one in the room who thinks to tip the hardworking band as everyone leaves around 10:30 p.m. Moving swiftly after such a long time sitting, I am eager to see if I can spot the stars of the Southern Cross from our rooftop room. I have always loved astronomy and this latitude may provide a rare opportunity to see the legendary southern sky constellation.[*]

---

[*] Alas, the sky is too cloudy.

Last Day

We are all hoping to reconnect with Rosa once more before we leave. In the short time we've been together we have developed a bond and affection for one another. Since we planned to have Javier transport us back to Quito, we asked if Rosa could join us for the long drive back, giving us more time to visit. (This is a first for Rosa to request the same of us, so we feel quite honored!)

Around one p.m. Javier and Rosa pick us up outside our hotel. Rosa is crying. She tells us that she had asked her new boarders from England if she could just leave dinner for them, allowing her to accompany us on the two-hour journey. The answer was, "No," they wanted dinner cooked and served to them. We are appalled! In great sadness we drop Rosa off at the *Supermercado* (large grocery store) in order for her to get the necessary dinner provisions. She will walk back to her home with the groceries. Carly offers, "I will write to you." To which Rosa responds, "Everyone always says that and nobody ever does."[*]

We return one last time to Rosa and Javier's house to retrieve the rest of Carly's things. During our initial stay with them there was no opportunity to view the infamous "electrical shower" so it is imperative I see for myself what Carly had described in such laughing horror.

Oh my God! it is just as frightening as Carly had portrayed! Attached to a lever *inside the shower* are bare wires that twist and turn around exposed pipes leading to a small water tank. It looks like an Alcatraz executioner's cast-off.

---

[*]   We did write but never got a response. But then again, the mail service there can be very unreliable.

Carly's modus operandi:

Turn on the water first. With trembling hand pull lever down to turn on the electricity. "I was too scared to do this and would yell for the Australian guy—who I had mistakenly thought was brave—and with his hands shaking, he would quickly swipe the lever down." (Looks like Rosa will have to help me the next time, she cynically deduced.)

"After adjusting the nozzles at not too low a pressure and not too high, you know the heater is working when you hear a hissing sound. Then you pray for the duration of the shower you don't die. You are supposed to turn the electricity off the moment you are done, but touching the controls with wet hands is petrifying to me so Rosa let me keep it on until she could get there. Sometimes while in the shower a spark or snapping sound happens and the electricity would turn off and you needed to work at turning it back on again or endure a freezing cold shower. Usually I would endure the freezing cold shower or just decide maybe I can wait another few days to bathe or, worse yet, it really isn't that necessary to rinse out all that greasy hair conditioner."

Stepping outside into the courtyard, I catch sight of a mysteriously dark figure in a black scarf and long black dress who, with gnarled fingers, is unlocking the entry gate. (The main entry gate is called *el portón*.) The woman is one of the compounds residents who owns a tiny grocery store, run just street-side. Whenever a patron is in need of service a bell is rung from outside the locked and caged store, alerting the proprietors of a customer. The customer explains what they want and the owner gets it for them, so there's no chance of shoplifting. All throughout Ecuador we run into this anomaly: tiny one-room stores, consisting of groceries and sundries secured behind a caged front, with only a small slot through which to pass procured items and money (like a jail cell). Rosa, Carly informs, makes use of this neighborhood store only for last-minute items such as bread or milk; her major shopping is always done at the *Supermercado* in Otavalo city.

Before long it is time to go and we pile back into Javier's taxi/car. The only notable experience to take place in the two-hour drive back to Quito happens while waiting in a ten deep, six lane, road toll stop. Here there are numerous vendors meandering about the cars, hawking their wares: newspapers, beverages, snacks, cigarettes, etc. Carly hails a woman for bottled water. Before our addled brains can say *Waaaaaaaiiiiiiiitttttt!* she opens it and gulps down a giant swig. We had been clearly warned to beware of refilled water bottles, *to listen* for the energy release when opening a new bottle since local tap water can result in severe abdominal consequences. "Carly did you hear the cap make a *psssssst* sound when you opened it?" I inquire. "I DON'T KNOW I CAN'T REMEMBER!!!!!" she wails. Ugh! What a blunder! Courtney and I are miserably thirsty too but with great fortitude, self-discipline, courage and valor, we resist partaking of the open container. (You and your gurgling, petri dish stomach are on your own with this one Carly.)

Isolation Is Not Isolated

That Rosa suffered from depression came as a surprise to me. As I wax on and on about the interconnectedness of developing world societies, it never occurred to me that a housewife in Otavalo, Ecuador would suffer from what I thought of as a modern Western syndrome: an isolated mother saddled with the task of raising children predominately alone. Having been in the situation, I have often thought that isolating a mother with children is the most unnatural of conditions considering our social make-up and our natural history of extended clan. Like the chimpanzees or the wolf pack, we are wired to the core as social beings; we need our tribe. To isolate one woman within the confines of four walls with clingy, completely dependent, warring, mewling and puking little creatures (children) is, well, you can't even call it *primitive* because I doubt even they did that. (It was contrary to professional consensus as far back as Australopithecus; I'll bet even *Lucy* had help.)

That Rosa's marriage was on shaky ground didn't help either. On Carly's days off, just as she was about to depart for the day, Rosa would *beseech her* to stay home and just *talk to her;* Carly would usually acquiesce. During these sessions she spoke of the difficulties of her relationship with her husband (a universal theme), the weight of their relentless economic pressures, and the loneliness she feels at the separation from her relatives who lived quite some distance away. She confided her dreams of opening her own restaurant someday, when the children were older, and of gaining some much sought after independence.

The one respite they had for stress-relieving entertainment was the occasional weekend trip to the *discoteca* (discotheque) for a night of drinking and dancing. This popular activity is rife with potential peril and, I imagine, not many seatbelts or designated drivers. Carly, who likes to dance but not drink, tells of one particularly harrowing evening accompanying them to a *discoteca*. After mucho drinking the evening drew to a close around three a.m. Carly (thoroughly exhausted by 1:30 a.m.) was then coerced into driving them all home on the completely unfamiliar, dark and twisting, Pan American Highway—full of other inebriated tavern patrons returning home. Adamantly protesting her ability to do this, she finally resigned herself to "give it try" after so much coercion.

The car was completely full: Rosa, Javier, Javier's brother and sister, plus the Australian roommate. With no power steering, the extremely stiff, decades-old, stick-shift, lurched and pulled, and was negotiated with great difficulty under Carly's tremulous hands. "Speeding cars were everywhere," Carly recalls, "people driving crazy, exiting bars, on the Pan American Highway in South America—**AT NIGHT!**" She was terrified! Upon reaching walking distance of home base, she attempted to bail (even though it meant walking eight blocks all by herself in the dark) since Javier's brother and sister still needed to be taken home another hour and a half away! Exiting the car Carly's resolved to remove herself from the perilous situation. Unfortunately, at this point Rosa begins crying and frantically begs and pleads Carly **not to leave her alone with her husband** who, drunk and slurring, is now pressed into driving duty; she needs help keeping him awake! Carly looked to the Australian guy for some kind of moral support, perhaps an offer to walk her home, but finds none. In ill-considered sympathy, Carly re-entered the car as a passenger, essentially placing herself into jeopardy just as much as the rest of them. Poor decision-making! IN RETROSPECT (we're only good at retrospect in our family, **never on-the-spot quick thinking**) Carly never should have caved to the pleading! But thank God they made it.

I heard about the entire escapade in a phone call the next day, mercifully *after the fact*. "Mmmmmmmmooooother! You will not believe what I did last night!!!"

Puerto López

Our plane departs at 7 p.m. from Quito (central Ecuador) for the first part of our journey to reach the Pacific Coast village of Puerto López. We arrive at the coastal Manta Airport at 8 p.m., dark.

Now I Know What Bait and Switch Means

Having read all the warning literature about Ecuadorian travel, a specific caution stood out about not accepting just any taxi ride outside airports: Have airport personnel call a ride for you. *Yeah, right.* When you're in the situation it is not that easy. As I approach airport personnel to do just that they point to a mass of taxis eager for us to take one tiny step outside and give me a look, like, *Are you blind lady?* Once we exit the building we are hit with an onslaught of competitors clamoring to get our business. With the previous warning in mind, I at least try to carefully scrutinize the options: No, not that one, he's too muscular and full of testosterone. That one looks a little suspicious and has too much product in his hair. Now, that one is well-groomed in dress shirt and khakis, a little bit pudgy and soft looking; that's good, we might be able to take him if we have to. *Sooo,* we make our choice: the pudgy, khakis guy. Once selected, he lets out a piercing whistle and up zooms a taxi from the business he's fronting. Before we can say *wait a minute*, our luggage is thrown in the trunk and we are off down a dark road with a nefarious looking stranger.

Oh boy, I'm thinking, we just violated every rule about getting a taxi at night. I'm hoping we are not killed at the edge of town or sold into white slavery. (*Very white* in our case, I wonder if there is a special section for that?) Seriously, our driver's overall demeanor does not make me relax. He seems a bit sketchy. I study the back of his lightly oiled, wavy haired, combed-back head. He appears to be approaching 50, of medium build, not particularly well-groomed. I catch the stale whiff of a recently-smoked cigarette. Carly, ever our translator, is in the front seat as he proceeds to tell us his life story, partly in English, mostly in Spanish. I remain wary...

Filled with trepidation, we head inland on a curvy, mostly deserted road. *Weren't we supposed to follow along the open coastline?* I thought. I begin imagining the armed and fortified hacienda where he delivers dumb gringas. "Now, how long will it take to get to Puerto López?" I ask, attempting to establish a rapport, as though the question itself will make him follow that route.

(Driver contemplating: *Oh, I was going to kidnap and torture them, but now that she mentions it, that drive to Puerto López is kinda nice …*) His actual response: "It takes at least two hours Señora." Ugh.

And they were very long hours.

After traveling inland for some 25 minutes, we finally head out along the coastal road. I breathe a sigh of cautious optimism. At least within sight of the ocean I have some assurance we are following the correct course. But now Courtney and I are lurching in the backseat with every sharp coastline curve. Naturally there are no seat belts. We remain wide-eyed and alert, as though *our* sharp attention will help our driver stay on this most precipitous road. As he becomes more animated with his stories, he gesticulates wildly while pointing out areas of interest. We come upon a treacherously high, steep curve above the ocean and **neither of his hands are on the wheel**! We three simultaneously break into a chorus of high-pitched screaming to jolt him back to reality! He seizes the wheel to correct our ocean-bound trajectory. *Pay attention to the road!* I silently plead. *Enough with the distracting stories!*

The entire taxi ride is a harrowing experience.

As we begin to comprehend the modus operandi here in Ecuador, we soon realize the concept of my lane and your lane is simply not in Ecuador's shared consciousness. Apparently the entire road belongs to the one with the most cojones. At one point on this drive we have three cars in our dark single lane. First there's us, then the one passing us, and then another one passing the guy passing us. I wish I were kidding. Numerous times our driver leisurely weaves around blind curves on the *opposite side of the road*. I'm hoping (more like praying) this seasoned driver knows what he's doing.

In the open fields along the side of the road, the headlights occasionally land on wild burros a precarious few feet from our vehicle. I've never seen loose, wild burros before. As I was thinking about burros as a potential roadway danger, a large dog suddenly jumps out of the blackness and lands directly in front of our taxi! Our driver slams on the brakes just in time to miss the wretched creature! Agh! A split-second, blessedly-averted bloody trauma! We all break into relief-applause—once we get back into our seats—and praise him for his quick reflexes!

As an added bit of local color, throughout the drive our cabbie nonchalantly points out the several white crosses placed in memory of those who met their deaths on this treacherous coastal road. One, he explains, involving an entire busload of touring international students that had plunged over the edge. Friends and relatives still make an annual pilgrimage to the site, he continues. *Please, oh please, stop sharing these stories.*

Once or twice we pass through a lovely and prosperous-looking seaside town or resort. I smell and feel the pleasantly warm, moist, ocean air. Peering out the backseat window, I begin to feel encouraged at our prospects. I see upscale hotels, fountains, palm trees, expensive cars, and so on. But we pass right through them and continue on into the black night.

Further down the coastal road, along remote stretches of highway, I am surprised and captivated by the unique spectacle of bamboo huts on stilts, all aglow on the landscape—kind of like Christmas tree ornaments. Lit from within, the fissures between the bamboo-slat walls emanate the florescent light of modern day electricity and have the effect of casting a halo of light around the primitive dwellings. At times they appear to be suspended in mid air. Very surreal. *Is that the blue light from someone watching television within this one room hut?*

Just before reaching our destination of Puerto López, we pass through a most unique tree canopy. Specifically grown and trained to envelop the roadway, we are immersed for a mile or so within a tree tunnel. The entire roadway is entombed by a low arch of dry, gray branches. Within the black of night, the solitary beams of the car headlights illuminate only the curved ceiling and winding path, creating the sensation of continually falling into a black hole. It's so mesmerizing and mysterious, and so easy to imagine a Harry Potter-like owl silently gliding along with us. We are all transfixed by this strange illusion.

Around ten p.m. we finally reach our long-desired destination of Puerto López. It looks about as inviting as a garbage dump. A mostly abandoned street scene consisting of a few loitering cantina patrons and a string of dismal *mercados* (stores) and everything in sight covered in a film of road grit. And in which of these dilapidated hovels do we have our reservations, *Carly?* I wonder while perusing the incredibly forlorn scene. The three of us are in a state of stunned silence and I am in a state of *prepared to panic.* Now, I am all for cultural authenticity, but I am also a mother with two daughters and safety concerns. Fortunately, we pass right through the shambles to a tourist-oriented hotel a mile or so up the hill where our driver stops.

The gated compound of our hotel appears to be absolutely beautiful and we breathe a great, collective sigh of relief. Perched on a bluff all by itself, our lodgings are all adobe, tile, and palm trees. Whew.

Before releasing us to freedom, our taxi driver makes a long-winded sales pitch about calling him for all our transportation needs while visiting Puerto López, including a ride back to the airport. Though we politely listen to his sales appeal—and he proves an honorable person after all—his driving skills left us speechless. So, the list of numbers he gives us makes it as far as the nearest waste basket the minute he is out of sight.

Due to our late arrival the hotel manager must open the office for us. He's an athletic, handsome guy dressed in chic sports apparel. He checks us in and hands over our key. Looking good so far; everything seems in order. *However,* the porter he calls to transport our luggage appears and he looks more like a recent parolee (Gruesome Murder One). He is tough and muscular, with beady-dead eyes, bristly hair and mustache, a face that would be an easy fit on any MOST WANTED poster. Though I concede he may be the nicest person in the world, WE DO NOT HAVE THE LUXURY OF TIME TO FIND OUT!

The wholesome-looking manager disappears while our new unsmiling companion hoists our bags. It is ink black outside under a murky, heavy and humid cloud covering as he slowly leads us to our room. We follow along manicured walkways, beyond an aqua-lit swimming pool, past the closed hotel café, around shadowed corners. All the while he remains stone cold mute. The only sound is an intense pulsating, throbbing hum of jungle insects (and my heart). The entire compound is dark and deserted; presumably, if there are other *living* hotel guests, they are all tucked away in their beds, sound asleep. Finally, reaching our corner room, we flick on the light switch to find our accommodations to be spacious and charming. Yay! And most fortunate of all, our porter leaves without killing us! (It's the little things ...)'

Courtney quickly lays claim to the top bunk bed and Carly and I take the comfy double.

My first intention is to check all the room's security features. Hmmm, no inside bolt, just a locked door with many available keys. No good. One of the three, large, crank-opening windows has a clearly broken latch (I report this, but it is never fixed). Though exhausted, I busy myself with dragging the heavy chest of drawers *screeching* against the floor tile smack against the door. Then I creatively pile all our luggage on tables against the curtains of the triple windows. At least if a *male*factor attempts to break-in we will hear plenty of clamor to warn us and thereby engage in high-decibel screaming. Eventually, both girls plead with me, "Mother just go to sleep!" But not until I feel all sufficient precautions have been taken. I leave one teeny tiny bathroom window open for much-needed fresh air, but only after carefully scrutinizing and determining that only a very slight and wispy Houdini-like guy would have any chance squeezing through ... and he'd be sorry if he did.

The following morning we awaken to a blissful, glorious array of color and light. Our airy room features a large bamboo ceiling fan, cream-colored adobe walls, terra cotta tiled floors and an immensely appealing, vivid blue-tiled bathroom. The blue shower, circular and spacious, glows beneath a skylight. The bathroom décor is so artfully and colorfully done, from exposed wood beams to the complementary burnt-orange walls, as to be worthy of a watercolor painting.

---

*   Thinking my fearful instincts may have been way off, I asked the girls their thoughts: Both agreed on his *silent, eerie vibe.*)

Deep Dot Thought

What is that unidentifiable, illogical appeal of imperfect craftsmanship? Though some of the bathroom hand-painted tiles were irregular and imprecisely aligned, it is that mark of human touch, the clear sign of a creative soul or *personality* behind it that makes it so charming. (Compared, say, to the machine precision of a Holiday Inn room, though that predictability certainly has its upside as well!) The elements that make up the room's basic materials seem to come straight from the earth, ocean and culture from which they emerge. The end result has such a great organic feel and tangible creativity.

But, there is a fine line between culturally charming and maddeningly dysfunctional.

Schizophrenic Bipolar Shower

Though lovely to look at, our shower was clearly possessed. (Yeah, it had *personality* all right.) From scathing hot to glacial cold, the temperature swung wildly no matter how delicately or minutely we attempted to manipulate the controls. Intermittent bursts of screaming poured forth from the shower as each of us in turn—alternately scalded and frozen—vainly attempted to subdue its diabolical behavior. (I reluctantly admit to an initial sense of false pride with the temp controls. I thought *My incompetent, ham-fisted daughters clearly do not possess my superior life skills, my finer dexterity.* How quickly the mighty fall!) By the third day, "Just leave it on when you find the right spot!" I screamed to Courtney. "Then I'll just jump in."

To no avail. Somehow sensing our plan, it would neither be deceived nor trifled with; the temp swung as erratically as ever.

In the end *malo espíritu* prevailed (9-0). We remain, humbly defeated.

AFTER A BLACK NIGHT FACING OFF FEARFUL DEATHS (whether by taxi, intruder, or porter), the extraordinarily bright, morning light of our compound never looked so good! Stepping outside into the yellow sunlight, we find the hotel is painted in vivid hues of yellow-gold, blue, pink and green, and landscaped with palm trees and spiky tropical plants. Potted red geraniums and fuchsia-flowered shrubs energize the light-play off the cobalt blue sky. Faux-adobe walkways curve and swirl into incredibly creative arches, nooks and crannies; art tiles of local flora and fauna are embedded in the alcoves. It is sensually overwhelming, visually stunning. Surveying the tropical luxuriance we are pleased to find all is well-maintained, well-manicured and, well, perhaps *a little too perfect* and made to please *los turistas*. However, in contrast to our scare from the night before, we are not about to complain. We will gladly accept tourist artifice over authentic peril.

Before we can begin our day in earnest, our family dermatologist warned us that every day, without fail, we need to slather sunscreen upon one another from head to toe lest our predominantly Scandinavian skin meets any equatorial sun (*yes, even under our clothes, she said*). Our travel doc said the same about high potency insect repellents. The practice of this advice, however, challenges our familial sense of modesty: we have never been a naked family. So this is all rather new. In fact, my Catholic upbringing taught me it was sinful to be naked *under your clothes*. (Yes, that's true. The devil resides in all the nooks and crannies.) Each and every morning the three of us have to perform a ritual of applying massive amounts of sunscreen lotion, followed by massive amounts of insect repellant onto one another's netherlands. It is somewhat liberating and comical as we dutifully line up, back facing back, like grooming baboons. (Or perhaps more like orangutans in our case considering the red-headed gene!)

Re: It's also a sin to think of us naked.

By the time we are ready the sun is blindingly yellow-bright by 9 a.m. when we meet for breakfast at the café's poolside table. Nearby are meticulously groomed, green topiaries sculpted into various sea creatures like whales and sharks. From this vantage, our hotel on the hill possesses a stunning view of a mostly wild, uninhabited coastline. We can see far beyond the dense, green, jungle foliage below, out to the deep blue ocean distance.

81

Hundreds of scavenger birds circle over an outlying shore, hungry for remnants cast from the morning fishing boats.

We are feeling anxious to maximize our time of only three days here. Carly takes the lead in organizing our events equipped with her *Lonely Planet* guide book, as well as some advice from her traveling friends. Atop the list is to partake of the whale watching excursions for which the region is well known. Scheduling this involves booking a daylong boat trip to the *Isla de la Plata* (Silver Island), promoted as "the poor mans Galápagos Islands." After whale watching is accomplished it is our intent to visit an indigenous community and archeological site (because we like that kind of stuff) located a few miles inland within the tropical dry forest of the *Parque Nacional Machalilla* (Machalilla National Park). And then, at some point, we'll take in *Los Frailes* (The Friars) beach, known for its exquisite, isolated beauty and excellent swimming. That should be enough to give a basic game plan for our three days.

Enter *Roberto*

Thus planned, our first order of business is to secure a ride into the city and formally make arrangements. The hotel provides a "taxi" service and calls a *motocab* for all our transportation needs. Here begins a wonderful relationship with Roberto, our jovial, delightful driver.

A motocab is a motorcycle (somewhat sputtering and old in our case) customized to pull a two-wheeled, three person carriage. Our canvas carriage is a bright yellow-gold with navy blue and purple trim, pulled by a cobalt blue motorbike. Roberto has painted the names of his three children, Evelyn, Diego y Emely in bold letters on the back (I guess to remind him who he's working for) and has a well-placed sticker of Jesus embracing three small children on the plastic window separating the driver and passengers. He appears to be in his mid-to-late thirties, mustachioed, of average height and build (say 5'8, 155 lbs.) and possessed of a gregarious, fun-loving nature. We like him immediately!

Stepping into the mostly open-air transport, the motocab itself is an adventure! A helmeted Roberto (his navy helmet looks like it came from the WWI era) in a cab-matching yellow-gold t-shirt, kick-starts the reluctant engine, and off we go careening down the hillside, buckshot gravel flying by the wayside! We all squeal with delight! There are no seatbelts and nothing but canvas between us and the open road. Why is this so fun? We are violating every safety rule we know! But, as is so often traveling in South America you must relinquish any semblance or delusion of control, toss all safety issues to the winds and *Vaya con Dios!* Letting go is such a liberating, if slightly insane thrill. (As long as nothing goes wrong.) Wheeeeeeee…eeeee eeeeeeeeee eeeeeeeeee!

In the light of the new day, we now see the roadway. Considered part of Ecuador's coastal highway known as *Ruta del Sol* (Route of the Sun) it is a well-worn, winding two-lane road, featuring spectacular ocean views, scruffy vegetation and, lamentably, a proliferation of roadside litter. I am taken aback by the sorry-looking vegetation nearest the roadway. It is besmirched in dust and seems to be suffering at best. The dry tropical landscape appears to be in basic survival mode: compact, reflective of and braced against some pretty harsh elements. But, we are visiting in the dry season. Perhaps another time of year would give a completely different impression? But it's still an extreme contrast to our familiar, rain-saturated and heavily forested, Pacific Northwest coast.

A less than fifteen minute drive brings us back into the village of Puerto López. The previous night's dusty main avenue is no more appealing in the daylight (though much less daunting) but with Roberto as our guide we find the most charming part of town a few blocks westward. Along the ocean front are about six or eight blocks of palm treed and prospering establishments: sidewalk eateries, ocean bars, and colorful shops all along an oceanside promenade known as the *Malecón*. On one side is a mix of various businesses, on the other several picturesque thatch and bamboo restaurants and bars (offering fresh fruit smoothies) right on the sandy beach. It is wonderful!

Our whirlwind village tour brings repeated bursts of horn honking from Roberto that pierce the air with his cheerful morning greetings. We sound exactly like the Roadrunner! Our gregarious driver liberally **bee bee beeps** his horn at every Tom, Dick and Harry ... errrrrr, Felipe, Diego and Hortensia in town. Clearly he is one popular guy! Most of the time we can't even see who he's honking at as we whiz past the open door business of a blackened, grease-laden mechanics garage; a *tienda* displaying colorful household items for sale (like multi-hued brooms in barrels beneath a weathered-red *Coca-Cola* street umbrella); and an adobe residence painted cobalt blue with black-barred windows, scratching chickens and single strands of dusty, hanging laundry.

Though the main tourist area is definitely charming, the rest of the village appears—to my middle-class Western eyes anyway—to be in struggling poverty. Ramshackle dwellings and small business enterprises scattered amid hard-packed dirt.

Roberto is intent on showing us Puerto López's sports stadium a little off the edge of town. Turning off the main road and onto a bumpy, twisty, primitive path we navigate through a windswept, trash-strewn field to get a good look at the structure. It is protected on all sides by a tall chain-link fence topped by barbed wire. The playing field (primarily used for *fútbol* or soccer) reveals trampled-down grass and drifting knolls of dirt. ESTADIO

PUERTO LÓPEZ is boldly printed on the overhang, sheltering the one, mid-size bleacher. The stadium is quite desolate looking. Or maybe it's the backdrop of the suddenly overcast sky and the barbed wire fencing that makes it all look so penitentiary-ominous? Nevertheless, it is remarkable a village of this size boasts such a large soccer stadium.

Done admiring the stadium we head back to the city to take care of business. This is boring: securing whale watching boat reservations (\$110), paying national park fees (\$60), and procuring cash from the sole ATM machine in town. During our three days here, at any particularly long lapse, Roberto takes off to enjoy camaraderie (*coffee? té?*) with his friends, but he always makes sure it is okay with us first.

Finally, we head north to visit the indigenous archeological site. Passing through the highway's tree tunnel in the daylight is a quite different experience than at night. Still an impressive canopy of overarching gray limbs, the daylight reveals a smattering of green foliage mixed in. We ask Roberto to stop and park so we can run out to the middle and stand in the center of the highway to take some photos ... *photos I'm sure no one has ever thought to take before.* Roberto seems to blush with a sense of local pride at our request and merrily acts as our watchman/photographer, as if in collusion with a criminal act: a stolen moment of us standing in the dead center of the highway.[*] *"¡Rápido, rápido señoritas!"* he laughs between passing cars, till we jump back in our carriage and off we go!

---

[*]   Possible valuable footage to be sent back to my husband documenting our moronic, untimely demise.

Banco de Pichincha and
The Only Cash Machine In Town

Boy, do we get to know this stretch of road from our hotel on the hill to Puerto López. On one of the days we painfully made the early morning trip three times when the town's sole bank and cash machine would not complete our transaction for the days needed cash. Returning to our hotel to retrieve *every credit card we had* (individually) until we finally determined the machine was broken, not, in fact, a problem with our cards.

By chance the ATM had a meltdown precisely during our first attempt at withdrawing money via a convoluted, bilingual transaction. We all tried our hand and failed, aware of a growing impatience simmering in the line behind us. The machine completely shut down and decided to hibernate on us! Guilt-ridden, and convinced it was we who had overheated it with our stressful, foreign commands—*maybe it just needs to rest for a while*— we made a hasty retreat out of town before we were found out.

(Imagined *Banco De Pichincha* mob reaction: "It was the pale gringas! Get a rope!" trailing on our dust plume.)

There was always a long line of disgruntled-looking customers waiting to use the cash machine. One morning, appropriately lined up like all ultra-queue-conscious Americans exhibiting our deeply entrenched, sheep-like adherence to the *standing-in-line code of honor*, we were aghast when two bodacious women popped out of a car and jumped right in front of us! A line we had been standing in for nearly a half hour! What gall, what chutzpah! Fortunately the locals waiting behind us were not at all amused either by their behavior and vociferously let them know it. (This is where I learned the f-word is truly universal.) The obnoxious women then backed off and got to the back of line with the rest of us. I'm guessing we foreigners are an easy mark for such aggressive tactics.

---

*   I had to laugh (shudder) when, during my time as an ESL teaching assistant, one of our adult foreign students was quite perplexed by the American propensity for "getting in line." He was puzzled: "Even when there are just two of you, you still make a line." It sounds pretty comical when you put it like that! One day he decided to perform his own experiment with Americans waiting-in-line (here's where *shudder* comes in) by

Parque Nacional Machalilla Agua Blanca
Manteña Comunidad

Traveling about seven more miles on the *Ruta del Sol* we reach the attractive wood sign designating the turn-off for *Parque Nacional Machalilla Agua Blanca Manteña Comunidad*. The string of unfamiliar words sends my brain into a flux of incapacitating, incomprehensible, incoherence. I become the incarnation of the word "nonplussed": a state of perplexity or bafflement preventing action, speech or thought—heavy on the thought. (This is true and not at all unusual. Come to think of it, I was *nonplussed* all through chemistry, biology and math.) My head is a vacuous *puna.** So I attempt to return as a sentient being by dissecting the sign's basic information. *Parque Nacional Machalilla* is the appellation of a 135,910 acre national park named for the pre-Columbian Machalilla culture. *Agua Blanca*, a small village of about 62 families, is named for the *white water* bubbling up from a volcanic source. And, finally, *Manteña Comunidad* or Community of Manteña signifies the indigenous culture that once thrived here and still maintains descendents.

Roberto tells us that the Agua Blanca village became of renewed interest when, about thirty years ago, a mudslide unearthed a burial site of the pre-Columbian Manteña culture. Excavations have since produced evidence of around 600 structures and make the area of great political significance as an urban and ceremonial center to ancient civilizations.

From the highway turn-off, a rough, dirt road winds upward another three miles through dust-choked and bleak looking vegetation—at least within the immediacy of the road. I spot a particularly dismal looking rest stop: a park bench made-up of dusty branches set within dry tinder—a bench I can't imagine anyone would ever want to sit on. At one point we have to stop and pay an additional entrance fee ($3 each) at the manned station (actually *wo*-manned and manned station occupied by a thirtyish *indígena* couple, casually attired in non-descript Western clothing).

---

choosing, as the lead car, to sit out a green light and wait until it turned red again, just to see what would happen. I suspect he learned the same universal truth I did (see box).

*   High Andes windswept, treeless wasteland.

The settlement of Agua Blanca lies amid some water-nourished tropical greenery. It is an attractive, primitive-looking assortment of a few thatched-roof buildings encircling an open area of reddish soil. The communal center consists mainly of a restaurant, small museum, tiny general store, souvenir stand, and a scattering of delightful looking dwellings. The handful of homes are made of bamboo cane and shade palm and adorned with wonderfully creative, curled-branch railings. Potted flowers adorn some of the decks, branch-ladders lean against the sides, and black hammocks are slung beneath the trees. Completing the picture are some heavily draped power lines, a few meandering chickens and, looking completely incongruous, a dry docked, large and sleek, modern motor boat. The only people evident are we tourists and a handful of guides.

All in all, it's a most pleasant, charming scene.

It is mandatory for all visitors be accompanied by an *indígena* guide throughout the tour. First, we are led to peruse the pre-Columbian artifacts gracing the tiny museum: ancient ossuary vessels with skeletons intact (the broken clay vessel containing a human skeleton brings to mind a giant cracked egg holding a frail, bird embryo); a rudimentary, stone power-throne said to be used by shamans or other spiritual leaders; ornate ceramics and necklaces; traditional tools like pestles and mortars, and an intriguing display of small clay faces, nose rings intact, that appear to be intentionally executed portraits of one another. The guide proudly points out the similarity of the ancient clay faces with photographs taken of the village's current residents.

Immersed within this somber tutorial atmosphere, we have to suppress our laughter when Roberto, attempting to clarify the custom of placing personal items like utensils and clothing in the ancient burial vessels, looks us over and whispers, "For example, the sunglasses on your heads would probably be included in your urns." (Funny thing to imagine unearthing ancient skeletons all with sunglasses perched atop the skull. "This group must be part of the same clan-of-the-weak-visioned. Probably of the Homohilfiger or Anthroakley genus.")

In numerous large jars along one wall we find several pickled and poisonous snakes preserved for our viewing pleasure. "Are these guys lying in wait for us on the flora and fauna segment of our tour?" I ask Carly to translate to our guide. "Oh no, Señora," he responds "they come out mostly at night!" Ewwwwwwwwwww!

At the end of the informative lecture, our *indígena* guide then demonstrates the raw musical power of the *pututos* (conch shells) traditionally used for long distance communication, trumpeting royal and religious ceremonies, offerings to gods, and as potent symbols of male fertility (kind of like muffler-less motorcycles and souped-up pickup trucks do nowadays). The conch sound is a surprisingly robust and resonant blast that succeeds in awakening our lulled senses from a semi-catatonic state—as only museum talk-tours can induce.

Basically educated, we head out to view the in situ excavation site. Walking over a rustic wooden bridge and through the jungle foliage, it does not take long to reach the thatched-roof protected dig. The quiet, isolated setting exudes an intriguing, primal atmosphere, draped in vines and abutting a steep ravine. Stepping down to the exposed embankment I feel a definite "in awe" moment gazing at the half-excavated, burial urns. Here are the carefully placed remains of a real human being ... existing ... breathing ... over a thousand years ago. A forever untold story of a life lived, of heartbreak and joy, of perhaps a beloved family member ...

(Of course it could've been the remains of a curmudgeonly, lecherous relative who nobody liked anyway. Here Lies Icky Uncle Kaopectate: *good riddance*. But that kind of destroys the moment.)

Nearby, there are building remnants to explore, most consisting of mere outlines from recent excavations. Notable is a long temple structure, fronted with posts of ornamental carvings.

After some time allowed for quiet contemplation, our guide then leads us through an informative nature walk highlighting local flora and fauna like banana trees, iguanas, giant termite nests, and one sighting of a colorful, blue-crowned *motmot* or clock bird, so called because it possesses a lengthy tail extension that switches like a pendulum. Surreal. Wild-eyed goats and a family of pigs startle and rush past us on the trail, a mad frenzy of squealing, fleeing little piglets of many colors.

Of particular interest is a specimen of the Ceiba (SAY-ba) tree. The multi-spine trunk is enormous, green in color, and distinctively capable of photosynthesis. The long trunk above the buttressed base was used to make canoes by the region's aboriginals, who were known for their far-reaching seafaring skills stretching from Peru to Panama. (The river running through Agua Blanca gave them navigable access to the sea.) Sadly, the coastal area of Ecuador was once rich in forests of these magnificent trees, our guide informs, and most of the (scrub) foliage we see is second growth.

Further on we chance upon some villagers washing their clothes in a small river. Now this is exotic! Through the foliage below us and in a protected ravine, we are close enough to hear convivial chattering among a small group of villagers. In stark contrast to the muted green, dry forest landscape, intense color splashes of bright red, orange and blue clothing lie upon the rocks and hang over branches erected just for that purpose (an environmental clothesline). A boy of about eight spots us on our elevated trail, hops on a boulder and cheerfully waves up to us. Of course, we genially return the wave. Chest out, he then proudly poses for a photograph. The others in his group simply ignore our presence and continue on with their visiting and laundry duties, probably inured to this common intrusion. Our guide comments that the families that make up the Agua Blanca community maintain a lifestyle similar to that of their Manteña ancestors.

We cross what was once a large river, today a wide, dry, river bed. I find this interesting as our guide attributes this extreme dry condition as a likely consequence of global warming; the rains are not what they used to be, he claims. The thriving green foliage and trees we do see, he explains, are the result of an underground water source still following the old river pathway. Once he draws our attention to this observable fact, the enhanced greenery winding beside the carved ravine is clearly evident. The situation is worrisome, he continues, because they do not know how long the underground source will continue to supply their land with sufficient water.

The mile or so long tour ends with a lovely-to-look-at sulfurous pond. The quiet reflective pool is surrounded by large leafy palms, the very attractive curly-branch fence, plus a nice deck on which to stand. Though *lovely-to-look-at* the water's sulfuric source smells strongly of rotten eggs. We are not inclined to take a dip though many visitors take advantage of the offer. The warm water provides a popular spot for locals to swim and bathe, after caking up with the pool's purportedly therapeutic mud. (A nearby lean-to conceals their privately stored soaps and shampoos.)

Machalilla National Park

As usual, until I visit a region I blatantly show my ignorance about its issues. Though I was not enamored by the aesthetic qualities of the dry tropical forest I learned these unique forests are in great peril. The park was established in 1979 to protect what little remains of the natural resources unique to the area.

> The flora and fauna of Ecuadorian Dry Forests are characterized by having acquired certain physiological-adaptive characteristics that allow them to survive extreme conditions of temperature and dryness. The forests of this eco-region are considered one of the areas of the world that are most at risk of biological extinction as the result of deforestation, agriculture and urban expansion, among the principal causes. It is estimated that Ecuadorian Dry Forest has been reduced to one percent of its original range, and much of the remaining forest is degraded.
>
> One in five plant species in Ecuador's coastal dry forests can be found nowhere else on Earth. Most all native trees lose their leaves in dry season. There are several species of kapok trees (ceibas), which have special adaptation: when the tree is young it develops thorns around its trunk that protect the water it harbors inside it from animals. When the trees are mature, they lose the thorns.[5]

Though it is only about the size of Oregon, Ecuador is considered one of the most diverse regions in the world. It is estimated that Machalilla National Park supports more than 270 bird species alone.

That Parque Nacional Machalilla exists at all is testament to contemporary efforts to safeguard the precious little that is left of the natural eco-system, and the educational role that the natives play in eco-awareness, protection and reforestation—reintroduction of native species is part of an ongoing environmental movement. (We observed numerous plantings of staked and wire-protected kapok trees.)

Ever since visiting Lima, Peru and learning about *la garua*, the seasonal fog that nourishes plant life adapted to such harsh coastal conditions, I find the phenomena here fascinating. The idea of a moisture-scarce ocean coastline seems so counterintuitive to me coming from Washington State's Pacific Northwest.

> The climate of this zone is directly related to the presence of the cold Humboldt Current and the warm El Niño and Panama currents. An important source of moisture in the hills and mountains is the sea mist known as *Garua* that forms during the austral winter, which condenses on trees and drips to the ground.
>
> The broken Andean landscape, the vast Amazon basin, the warm El Niño current, the cold Humboldt current, the Torrid Zone and the unique variety of ecological layers characterize the present territory of Ecuador as the scene of continued, widespread and complex cultural interactions that have lasted over 10,000 years.[6]

Los Frailes Beach

Back down the hill and but a few miles away, still within the borders of Parque Machalilla, we spend the afternoon at this utterly exquisite, remote beach of golden sand and aqua water. Less than ten people share this isolated cove with us.

But first, to protect our sensitive skin, Roberto is determined to score a *sombrilla* (beach umbrella) from an acquaintance of his that we go miles and miles out of our way to procure, nearly returning to Puerto López. Finally reaching the beach, planting the antiquated umbrella in the sand, it takes about three seconds for the strong beach winds to reduce it to its skeletal remains (yes, we paid money to rent this). The singular flapping fabric left hanging by a thread provides a five- to-nine inch span of moveable shade that blusters around like a wild banshee. Our despair quickly turns to laughter at the utterly ridiculous spectacle, at the unfolding folly of best laid plans.

I intend to hold the fort down—anchored by our rented shade-stick—of discarded clothes and towels while the girls go for a swim. They appear to me like cavorting porpoises lolling and frolicking, bouncing and flipping amongst the challenging push and pull of the waves. They even stand on their heads in a simultaneous show of untapped Groszhans talent: four lily-white legs wiggling up to the sky. Their incessant terror, exhilaration, shrieking at each oncoming wave fills the air and mingles with the rolling, roaring, powerful surf. They are having a ball!

They ask me to take a photo of them with their camera and because I'm old I accidentally shoot a video. (These new-fangled camera/phones do everything nowadays, save self-administered medical procedures: PRESS 2, SELECT COLONOSCOPY, INSERT APP, PRESS ENTER.) However, this accidental footage proves to be extremely entertaining. I don't know if I can translate the humor or not, but I'll try: The foreshortened images on the video make it look as though the two of them are incessantly shrieking, panicking, and spinning into a vortex … in about four inches of water about six inches from shore. We laugh uproariously reviewing the skewed-perspective footage of their rapidly rotating, sand-whipped bodies. (Imagined reaction of a passerby, looking on: "What's wrong with you two hysterical girls? Just roll yourselves over onto the beach!")

Strolling along the beach, luxuriating in the late afternoon sun, the warm water and powerful surf make for an extraordinarily pleasurable experience. At the end of the beach I write Mark's name in the sand of this distant shore, in gratitude for this most unique adventure.

… Later that evening, as we lie in our beds, journaling, musing, reflecting on the day's magical seashore excursion, from the top bunk bed issues the nascent stirrings of a hitherto unlooked for poetic writer: another Gabriela Mistral? Pablo Neruda? Isabel Allende?

> *"Itchy, itchy*
> *Scratchy, scratchy*
> *I've got sand*
> *in every cracky"*

One never knows what lurks in the heart of Courtney.

WE HAVE DINNER in downtown Puerto López. Thanks to Carly's *Lonely Planet* guide book we find the most charming open-air restaurant a half-block off the Malecón. Everything about it attracts us: a cheerful, hand-painted sign beckons atop a modest, thatched roof and bamboo pole exterior; golden light filters onto the sidewalk through a cascade of hanging tropical plants. Steps down lead onto a hard-packed earthen floor, the interior revealing rust orange tables of varying heights within a small but very cozy, cool room. The place exudes a bohemian quality; the look one imagines a quintessential tropical café (well, at least in my imagination).

An artfully designed poster board at the *restaurante* entrance offers several favored items like crêpes, salads, kebabs, Colombian coffee ("Real Coffee" it boasts!) and the clincher, vegetarian options. Perfect: All the *authentic local cuisine* we are so bold to sample … (sarcasm).

We start off with a round of very berry smoothies (everyone knows the native peoples loved their smoothies, traditionally made by a rapidly rotating pestle and mortar). So far so good. We enjoy watching the sidewalk parade of locals betwixt the insanely thriving ferns. The only other patrons are a twentyish couple at a back table, befitting the ambiance: unruly long, brown locks, *inteligente* in looks, accessorized with a plethora of beads on black leather strings. They must be engaged in some esoteric literary discussion, I presume, perhaps weighing the merits of *realismo mágico* (magic realism).

"So, do you think Cameron Diaz is getting too thin?" a snatch of conversation floating from *our* table.

Although Courtney had subscribed to vegetarianism for several years, she had recently resumed her carnivorous ways. Carly maintains a strict vegetarian diet and I straddle the fence, making an honest attempt to curb my carnivorous appetite and become a more enlightened human being. Though the kebob is very tempting, I decide to order a vegetarian plate along with [saint] Carly. Courtney goes for the kebob.

Our giant plates come. Carly's and my plate are heaped with boiled and overcooked vegetables (mostly soggy broccoli) over brown rice. Courtney's plate is heaped with marinated beef, tomatoes and onion sizzling on skewers, and hand-cut, delectable french fries. Ours is hideous. Courtney openly luxuriates in every bite. (No, she does not share; I have the fork wounds to prove it.) "That's what you get for ordering vegetarian," her unsympathetic commentary. "And don't touch my plate." We try to like ours—really we do, but it is not possible. Eventually, toward the end, a few french fries are tossed our way.

As we embark on our motocab ride home, feeling like queens chauffeured around in a carriage, Carly announces to Roberto, "Take us home our king." A group of sociable, young men, overhearing the command, chime in, "WE WANT TO BE YOUR KING!" We all enjoy a moment of light-hearted laughter together.'

---

* In the early evenings all along the Malecón, a very bizarre sight was that of a **massive amount of birds** (swallows I believe) solidly packed, shoulder to shoulder for several city blocks, completely weighing down the heavily-draped power lines. I've never seen anything like it. It was kind of eerie, all of them snoring and oblivious to the traffic noise below.

The Boat Ride
(One Paternity Verified)

Puerto López is a well-known destination for whale watching from the months of June through September. Humpback whales come up from Antarctica to mate and calve off their warm coastal waters, leaping into midair to the gasps and wonder of all paying tourists. For once, we happen to be in the right place at the right time! So you'd think this would be perfect ... wouldn't you?

We (Carly) make reservations with one of a plethora of companies offering various package tours. Actual ad:

"YOU MAY SEE INDIVIDUAL WHALES, PAIRS OR SMALL GROUPS OF UP TO EIGHT, AND THE MASSIVE WHALES CAN BE OBSERVED JUMPING OUT OF THE WATER!"

WHOO HOO, that's for us! We barely hesitate to plunk down the spendy fee, reasoning, *When will we ever be back here for such an opportunity?*

Now, that morning around the breakfast table (this plays into the rest of the day) before we ever even left the hotel for our boat tour, we experienced a strange encounter of the third kind: Carly's common sense momentarily evaporated! Courtney and I were witness to the strangest gaffe I have ever heard her make ...

A kindly, elderly American couple moseys by our poolside table to engage in small pleasantries, offering, "Oh, you're American too, where are you from?" Followed by our congenial, "... and where are you from?" type of chatter. Upon learning their home state origin of ALABAMA, Carly uncharacteristically quips, "I didn't think *you people* even traveled." Laugh and wink.

Courtney and I gasp—in jaw dropping utter disbelief—at what we just heard come out of her mouth. The genteel Southern couple slightly hesitate (did I detect a flicker of "dis" recognition in their eyes?), graciously change the subject, and amble on.

"WHAT WERE YOU THINKING, CARLY!!!??" Our two shocked faces swivel around and lock onto hers. *What?* Her face innocently registers. This normally conscientious world traveler explains her errant comment as the result of her last few weeks of constant flippant repartee among her young co-workers of late. "CARLY, THAT DOESN'T CARRY OVER!!!"

Well. It's ironic and amusing to report that later we learn, though their home state was indeed Alabama, they had spent the last 30 years doing missionary work ... *in Africa.**

With breakfast behind us, the day starts out in a cheery way. Our golden-yellow motocab arrives with our always delightful driver; the glowing carriage awaits us on the threshold of our brightly-hued, faux-adobe hotel. The sky is an intense cobalt blue and everything in all directions is bright! bright! bright!

It all looks so very promising ...

This is a daily pattern. Each morning Roberto picks up his gringas, all shiny and new and clean like daisies, filled with anticipatory excitement about what adventures lie ahead. Nine hours later, he deposits three unrecognizable dirt piles, bedraggled and world weary, dragging various articles of soiled, limp and discarded clothing—looking as though we had been hog-tied and drug behind a horse for several low tide miles. (In weighty thanks to the layer upon layer of sunscreen and bug repellants that effectively magnetize all dirt particles within a five mile radius.) I'm not exaggerating (much)—we put in some extremely long, grueling days.

At the start of day, it is extraordinarily fun when Roberto—we three in tow—peals out of the hotel driveway and races off with a down-hill momentum from our lofty, touristy refuge. He is so fun-loving with a good heart and a twinkle in his eye—especially when he teases us! We enjoy him immensely.

---

* On the upshot though, Courtney and I do enjoy ~~torturing~~ gently reminding a deeply chagrined Carly of this revelatory fact. ("Shuuut up!" her continuous, painfully-weak defense.)

As we hug the ditch bank in our tiny transport it is not long before Roberto happens upon a fellow motocab driver struggling up a hill. *Bee bee beep* goes his roadrunner horn in a machismo challenge and they engage in a one-way chariot race, straining to pass each other at speeds approaching 17 mph. We invariably lose and breathe a sigh of relief when Roberto pulls back into our lane!*

The company offering our whale tour is located right on Puerto López's attractive promenade. After reporting in, we have ample time for brunch as we await various assortments of tourists to congregate from other hotels. Showing up for our *same exact* boat tour is the missionary couple that Carly so grievously (albeit unintentionally) offended earlier. We keep our eyes downcast and scurry away from them whenever possible.

We choose a restaurant with a second story balcony for our morning *batidos,* fresh baked bread, orange juice, pancakes, eggs, and the omnipresent *Nescafé.* It would be picture perfect—refreshing tropical street scene below overlooking the *Malecón,* and situated directly across the street from the stunning ocean view—except that from a building three doors down, loud, dust-spewing construction is taking place, drifting over and onto my banana pancakes. As the backed-up truck's cement mixer churns and the resulting goopy concoction flows down the long funnel, a crew of about seven men labor like cogs in the gritty, hot process. Reggaetón and a crazy mix of American music blare from their weather-beaten, mud-encrusted stereo.† I study their work movements while they study

---

*   Losing despite Courtney's whipping out a metal spear—sparks flying—to debilitate the competing motocab's wheels (we wanted to help Roberto out á la *Ben Hur*). We didn't care much for those snooty European tourists the other guy was hauling anyway. The look of *l'horror* on their faces was kinda fun.

†   There's always a crazy mix of English music with Latin American music overheard on radios (like in taxis). From American or English pop culture you will hear a playlist like: the Bee Gees *Shadow Dancing* followed by Chubby Checkers *Twisting the Night Away,* then the Beatles *Got to Get You Into My Life,* followed by Michael Bolton *How Am I Supposed to Live Without You;* all intermixed with Reggaetón and all the hits of Shakira (in Spanish). I've heard it said "this is where old songs go to die" and that does have a ring of truth. A song from Pitbull *I Know You Want Me* was really popular at the time of our 2009 visit. Michael Jackson had just died and we were happy to get away from the insane US 24/7 media coverage only to find an outpouring of Michael Jackson mania here as well. *¡Qué sorpresa!* (What a surprise!)

my fair-haired daughters whenever they can steal a furtive glance. (Yeah, I-THE-MAMACITA SAW THAT!) I can't imagine a more miserable occupation under the equatorial sun. I watch one of the underlings push a heavily-laden wheelbarrow toward the unsheltered, heat-radiating cement foundation; he is already drenched in sweat and it's not even noon. I can't imagine what it feels like at the end of the day, much less after repetitive mornings facing the same. What a hard way to make a living! [See box relating Mom's hard labor past.]

Just before the tour starts, we realize we are one bathing suit short (Courtney left hers in our Seattle airport hotel), so we do some last minute scurrying around to find a cheap, yellow polyester number that never really fit any of us—but somehow ends up on mom (more about that later).

Finally headed to our vessel, the beach scene is, to us, pretty exotic. My first encounter is that of a late fortyish *afroecuatoriana* (Afro-Ecuadorian woman) in a tattered straw hat, barefoot, sitting on an overturned bucket, slicing up a batch of bloodied fresh fish. She looks annoyed. Nearly all of the plentiful fishing boats around us are painted blue, some with white or blue green trim, intensifying further the naturally vivid bay colors. (Puerto López is known for their perpetually blue boats.) There's a bustling, chaotic activity all along the beach: seabirds (pelicans, frigates, vultures) trying to snatch morsels, fisherman marketing their catches, and we plentiful tourists crossing to our awaiting boats through a gauntlet of children trying to sell us everything from gum to water. The pint-sized entrepreneurs are very aggressive, but I am in a haze of new sights and sounds and slow to react to their nonsensical pitches (It's all Greek to me. "What are they saying, what are they saying, Carly?" as I politely shake my head to demonstrate *no comprendo*. "Just keep walking mother!" she yells as she unflinchingly slaps them aside … just kidding!)'

After traversing the beach, we must all wade into the surf to board our vessel. It is a very slippery, somewhat daunting process. Small waves lap *above* our knees, each of us carrying shoes and dry provisions above our heads as if in a Conga line. From the water we need to hop aboard a

---

* Carly has a lot of pent-up frustration from having to be patient and kind all year as a second grade teacher.

bobbing vessel while grasping a crewmate's extended hand. I'm hoping that the slick fiberglass surface does not result in an embarrassing and potentially injurious slip. **OW, DO I SMACK MY KNEE HARD!** as I slide right into one of the boat's raised fiberglass seats. I pretend not to feel a thing, envisioning the grotesque bruise already coagulating. Once safely aboard, we three carefully scrutinize the seating arrangement, scheming ahead to secure the best possible position to view all those flying whales.

Mom's Hard Labor Past
Historical Documentation for My Children

I have not entirely escaped nightmarish occupations. My worst experience of all—summer of '72 employment to fund college expenses—was that of loading and unloading hop vines in over 100 degree weather. (Yakima is the undisputed king of the nations' hop production.) Employees dressed from head to toe in protective clothing (including sweaty rubber gloves) to guard against the rash-producing, abrasive vines. I drove an antiquated truck, grinding all gears out to the fields and back to the processing plant; my indented, bent driver's door refused to stay closed and I constantly had to reach out of the lurching vehicle to bang it shut as I bumped along the jarring, rutted rows. Sweltering in the intense heat and not daring to open the windows for fear of the massive infestation (from some unsprayed fields) of humpbacked inchworms dropping from the 20 foot vines as though raining from the sky. I studied in horror as several squirmy individuals simultaneously humped up, then stretched their way across my windshield in grotesque annelid-burlesque. (Cue can-can music.)

The worst is yet to come. We had to unload our own trucks, standing on a high platform, grabbing each vine from the bed and attaching it to what looked like an overhead meat hook. When the harvested vines became entangled, it was necessary to *jump into the truck bed* to pull the wormy vines out and attach to the conveyer hook. Doing this, I felt as though I had died and gone to hell (I have an intense snake/any-wormlike-thing phobia. I don't even eat spaghetti.) Walking the plank, unsure what ghastly fate (if any) lay in store for me, I braced myself, essentially held my nose, and jumped in. My ex-friend who got me the "easy job of just driving a truck"—you know who you are Carol Deccio—pulled a worm from her ear as she stood on her platform right next to mine, waiting for me to re-emerge, all the while apologizing profusely for what she had gotten me into. (I often wondered how many of those worms made it into the beer.)

After each restless night of stressful hop-vine-worm dreams, both my arms would fall **dead asleep** (and I mean **dead)** and I would have to lay them in the bathroom sink each morning, running tepid water over them to awaken for the day's dawn-to-dusk operation. It was like having somebody else's Frankenstein arms. (The employer was an acquaintance in dire need of harvesting help, or I'd have quit.) I lasted 30 days and nights.

(My then boyfriend, Mark, helped me out one Sunday afternoon, declaring afterwards, "I wouldn't do this job for a million dollars." It's no wonder I married [him] for money.)

Now this is where—were I an honorable person—I would have grabbed a bullhorn to announce to all my unwitting co-passengers, "Do not, I repeat, DO NOT get on this boat **WITH ME** if you expect to see any sign of a whale! Save your money, jump ship and swim away like water rats from a sinking vessel and book another whale tour!"

All these new water-culture sensations immediately thrust me out of my comfort zone (*the temple of my familiar*). We—my entire female lineage of ancestry—are not any kind of water-boat people; it is alien to our natures. Known primarily to stay in the cabin by the fire (with a shotgun and some kind of home fermented brew by our side) no spouse or earthly force could ever pry us away from that hearth. I don't know how we ever got to America from the Old World … must've been a cabin perched on that ship somewhere, a water voyage unbeknownst to great-great-grandma, still rocking a weapon in her lap, warmed by the fire, sipping on a brew.*

So, clothes partially wet from boarding, it's time to strap on the damp life jackets as the boat rocks with the sparkling blue, sea waves. This is a rush in itself. I feel as though I am on the cusp of a great adventure!

Our boat mates consist of the elderly missionary couple, now joined by their thirtyish daughter and son-in-law, and their blonde, eleven-month-old baby. All of them sporting floppy, Gilligan-style hats. (I judge harshly: *Are you nuts taking a fair-skinned baby on this tour, under this brutal equatorial sun? He could bounce right off the boat and into a whale!*) He is already fussing and I imagine could conceivably be a wailing pain throughout the tour. Immediately, the entire family sets about mollifying him and his cranky outburst. They put to use the tiny tyke's preternatural ability

---

* The story goes that on one occasion when my grandfather was off fiddling somewhere (literally, he was a fiddler), Grandma LeMire saved the Minnesota homestead and the first five offspring from a herd of stampeding cattle by discharging her shotgun in the air (and the help of a trusty dog barking like mad in the hayloft). The sound caused the herd to split right down the middle and around the homestead. Family lore has it that she disposed of interior household rats with her shotgun too—at least in the basement. (What an illustrious ancestry, you're thinking, chock full of blueblood royalty!) Now, what if Grandma LeMire had been off kayaking? I wouldn't even be here.

to imitate sounds, shouting out various creatures like: dog (*arf!*), donkey (*heeeehawwww!*), goose (*honk!*), monkey (*ooh ooh ooh*), and strangely enough, car alarm. I can't think of a vowel string to mimic this but I'll try: *wee ooh wee ooh*, followed by the all-too-familiar, grating *egh egh egh egh egh*. That is the show stopper. The rendition is eerily spot-on. The kid is good. Vegas material if they could hold him at baby age.

Also from our hotel is a mother/daughter duo hailing from New Jersey. The dark-haired, 57-year-old Italian-heritage mother, sporting black, thick glasses—she is soft and old-fashioned in appearance—seems incongruent with her slender, tattoo displaying, hip and quiet daughter, probably in her early twenties, and now living in Oregon. All the more impressive, thought I, wanting to share a vacation with her mother (such as myself)! It is heartening and refreshing to see.*

There are three or four college-aged missionaries from competing denominations (Methodist vs. Baptists, I believe; stay tuned for the heated playoffs). This leads me to wonder: are there missionary wars out there competing for developing world souls? How does that play out on the ground? And which one really has *the one true message*. I hope there's no pulling of hair involved—especially involving the native: *This lost soul is mine to save! I saw him first! Go get your own!* Add to this mix the strengthening presence of Seventh-day Adventist and Mormon churches making major inroads into this predominantly Catholic country; it has all the ingredients, a perfect storm if you will, for a multi-denominational free-for-all.

Completing our group is a family of four, lean and sleek, European sophisticates, also staying at our hotel (*long, tall, tan, cold,* as Carly succinctly put it) consisting of a dark-brown haired, bronzed couple with matching dark-brown haired, bronzed teenage offspring. They speak to no one (yes, they clearly know English). We never could determine the identity of their native tongue, surmising it was some kind of unusual dialect (perhaps Basque or Catalan?). Whenever we spot them on our shared three-day holiday they appear to do everything humorlessly hard: precision pool

---

* Except for the fact that I was quite chagrined every time the reticent, marshmallow-looking mom kept right up with my *self-perceived* daring ways.

diving; mechanical snorkeling; expressionless sunbathing; and somber, rote-like dining: ne'er a smile crosses their tawny lips. Smartly, continentally attired at all times, you could tell they were European just by their clothing.' (I coveted the woman's hiking boots and slick khaki pants with the un-zipped half-bottoms kept coolly tucked *atop* her boots.)

Finally, off we go on our merry way, rolling and bouncing o'er wave after wave, lull after lull, crest after crest, sea spray in our face. Yeah! This is fun! Until I look over at Courtney. She's not having fun. She looks ghastly. She can't speak. Oh oh …

"I don't feel very well," meekly issues from an ashen, sap-green face. And over she goes, toppling onto my lap.

Henceforth begins four hours (two hours up, two hours back) of nauseating, life-cursing, stomach-churning, misery for Courts. It is, at that very moment, we discover she gets abysmally seasick just like her father! (Who we can now be sure is Mark. So it's kinda good news/bad news situation … kidding!) Then comes the surprising revelation that this is the very first time she had ever been on a boat trip. When I query her on this point, she snaps, "Just when do you think I've ever had a chance to go on a boat trip mother?"—inject dripping sarcasm here, especially on the word muth*eeer*. Ah, she can still be snippy, even in her weakened condition, still dissing me about the trips she's missed out on.

So, with this limp, damp body draped over my lap we go racing over the sea in our quasi jet boat, pounding the waves. Seated across from us, all in firing line order, every single passenger shoots a somber look our way, their faces registering a *better you than me* indifference as well as wariness at the unsavory prospect *their excursion* might be negatively impacted by the sight of human misery. (I don't blame them, this is an expensive jaunt.)

---

* What is it about that Euro-chic look? You can't quite put your finger on it, but there's a certain *je ne sais quoi* about those sweaters … those scarves … those swimsuits … that just look foreign … and trés chic.

Courtney's firsthand rendition: "When I was on that boat I felt my center of gravity just flop around. Everyone on the boat was staring at me to see if I was going to blow! Boom, boom, boom, over the tops of the waves! I was nearly airborne and you and Carly had to physically hold me down on that seat. Hot, sweaty, sick like I'm going to throw up any second and a crowd of 13 people staring at me. That's what I remember."

Carly wasn't feeling so hot either. In the first hour of our return voyage, she breaks: "I don't care about the whales anymore! I know I'm never going to see one and I just want to go back!"

Ah, all the cinematic potential in a Groszhans' international adventure, not unlike a scene from *Out of Africa*: the musical score soaring in a crescendo of violins, a slow, zeroing-in Meryl Streep close-up of anguished, frustrated ... green faces, intensifying the dramatic moment when we reach a life-defining revelation ... *crap, we should've just stayed home.*

Every few miles the boat captain cuts the engine so we can list and roll in the water indefinitely, and scrutinize distant, gray blips on the far horizon … blips that look suspiciously like gray waves instead of whales. *Was that a fleeting wave bump or a sleek whale hump?* **No one can tell**. You can imagine Courtney's appreciation for each one of these grievously prolonged delays. Everyone on the boat attempts to block out the spectacle of her tormented condition, scurrying to the far corners of the vessel. (I can't block her out 'cause she's draped over my lap.)

Eventually the missionary people decide to share some of their Dramamine with Courtney. "~~Not because they wanted to, but more likely because Jesus wanted them to," later commented a jaded, motive-wary Carly.~~

Four futile stops and two excruciating hours later we FINALLY arrive on the island. Carly and I roll Courtney onto the beach and up to the lone structure providing shade. It is a desolate looking outpost. A long open-air roof covers a gritty cement patio and offers the only shade under which we haggard-looking tourists have to congregate. The midday heat is stultifying; the bathrooms to die for (that is, you want to die for having to use them). There is a lone hammock upon which to rest if you could manage to balance on the three befouled strands that hadn't yet unraveled. Otherwise, it means sitting on the cement floor once all the white plastic chairs are taken. Bird droppings are on everything, which leads me to the explanation of the name *Isla de la Plata* or Silver Island. It is not known whether the name reflects the use of the island in the 1600s by Sir Francis Drake to tally his booty captured from a silver-laden galleon, or whether it reflects the massive amount of *guano* (bird poop) cascading down the cliff sides, giving the island a silver sheen. We are sitting amongst some major proof toward the latter.

Left asunder in this shelter for a questionable and unreasonably long period of time, our several boatloads of tourists languish in the midday heat, semi-suffocating for close to two hours as we wait for our guides to offer some guidance. *Where are they? What in the heck are they doing?* It was an odd delay.

> "[There was a] downtrodden look to the whole damn island. There
> were so many holes in the one hammock you couldn't even lie in
> it. Most everyone was uncomfortably HOT. We waited a long time
> on that concrete floor. Everything seemed dirty and the sun was so
> frickin' strong."
>
> — Courtney's fond reminiscence

Of course, our attention is focused entirely on Courtney's precarious state.
We roll her over to look at her face. It looks a little better. The long delay,
coupled with Dramamine, gave her time to partially recoup and regain
some degree of equilibrium. Now the basic quandary facing her is this:
go on a hot, yet potentially attention-diverting hike, or to stay behind and
fully concentrate on nausea-lingering misery? The lesser of two evils (at
the time) appears to be the hike.

AT LONG LAST the guides reappear and rejoin their charges, ready
to lead us to the trailhead. Resurrecting from our heat-induced comas,
we have to tackle a 600 foot elevation gain right from the get-go—one
miserable, long, wood stair-step at a time. I can usually tolerate such
exertion when there are at least some level spots (even an infinitesimal
switchback) upon which to replenish one's reserve and to push off from.
However, a steep staircase with no landings—in this kind of heat—is, for
me, the most hellacious of tasks. After less than ten steps my chest begins
to burn and ache in a gasp for oxygen, my head pounds with my throbbing
heart, and sweat cascades in salty rivulets down my face and back. At the
same time I feel pressure to continue apace for fear of slowing down the
long line behind me. AND I DON'T WANT TO BE THE ONE TO
HOLD UP THE LINE! (*How is the elderly missionary couple managing this?* I
wonder. *Or what about that New Jersey Marshmallowmom?*) It is with some relief
to find that Carly's not managing any better. I don't have the stamina to
dare look at, much less approach, Courtney.

IT IS SO HOT AND DRY. I look for a redeeming sign of aesthetics
to emerge from the landscape. It doesn't. What scant vegetation there
is, is dirty, scratchy, dry, and rough. Finally, after completing a multitude
of chest-burning Stairmaster hurdles we come upon a makeshift rest
stop, consisting of bound, scavenged branches, erected within a partially

vegetated hollow. The place is almost appealing. I feel a twinge of hope. (Alas, it is to be our last encounter with anything resembling living foliage.) The missionaries appropriately claim the lone bench beneath the sparse shade; the rest of us muddle around, awaiting our guides arrival.

Once they have cornered and corralled any wondering strays, the guides assume a directive stance. At this juncture there is a well-defined fork in the trail: a funky wood sign, leaning sideways into an embankment, shows a white painted-on arrow going UP and a flat horizontal arrow going left. It is explained that here we have the option to follow a longer, more rigorous upper island route, offering spectacular coastline scenery and a plethora of potential wildlife sightings such as sea lions, porpoises, sea turtles and some rare species of birds, or the lower, less strenuous route featuring mainly boobies and frigates. Now, we don't really know what boobies and frigates are (well, not the bird kind anyway) but we have to reach a family consensus.

"There's no way in hell I'm going on the hard one," ~~mortally threatens~~ softly demurs Courtney.

"Either way is a scratchy miserable nightmare," ~~darkly portends~~ positively inputs Carly.

Well, I think we're all in agreement then. Though it is hard on my ego to take the easier, less-exciting route, the alternative scenario is just too horrible to contemplate.* †

---

* I know, I know, someone else writing this may well be waxing about the austere desert-like beauty and I feel kind of guilty about this. On the other hand, I need to *tell my truth;* and *my truth* was *ugly.*

† 2014 I feel a bit exonerated after painting such a dismal description of our "Poor Man's Galápagos Island" when I happened upon Charles Darwin's diary entry about Ecuador's real Galápagos Islands. (To find the Galápagos Islands follow the equator, as the condor flies, 570 miles due west from our Poor Man's island): "The stunted trees show little signs of life.—The black rock heated by the rays of the vertical sun like a stove, give to the air a close and sultry feeling. The plants also smell unpleasantly. The country was compared to what we might imagine the uncultivated parts of the infernal regions to be."[7] HA!

While we are dithering away in our oxygen-depleted state, eight, long, bronzed, European legs march right past us and charge up the hill in wordless lockstep. I'm not kidding. It is nearly inhuman: like human-sized copper-toned army ants. There is never any question about the course *they are taking*. Soon they are just little puffs of *über allen* (above all) dust on the horizon. ~~We all hope they don't see a thing; even the missionary people subtly curse them.~~

Okay, so now it's our turn. Our lower-route-group falls into: all the Baptist and Methodist missionaries; the Vegas baby; a few hedonistic looking yuppies from other boats; a recovering Catholic; an agnostic; and a bitter, resentful person of all the heinous damage missionaries have inflicted upon indigenous cultures over the centuries. I'm not saying who is what.

Punta Los Boobies (Boobies Point) No, I didn't make that up.

We proceed to slog along the dreadful trail, stopping only to marvel at nightmarish, convoluted plant specimens that somehow manage to survive in hellish conditions (like prickly and contorted Cactus Trees). As we're traversing atop the isle's tableland we have an open ocean view in the far distance (*is that a whale spout or sea spray? we're still confused*) and before long we come upon some strange birds nesting in the center of the trail. They have absolutely no fear of us. We all gather around our first sighting of a Blue-Footed Booby family: blue-footed parents with chicks that are fluffy, downy white, way-adorable creatures. Our group energizes like paparazzi chancing upon *Brangelina*, snapping a whirlwind of photographs from every conceivable angle. (*Geez, get a life*, wants to say the huddled booby family.) In a flurry, the other-boat yuppies activate some pricey, professional camera gear—lacking only a seasonal back-drop and flattering light spots. We are in sheer disbelief at the birds' *unflappable* complacency at our presence.'

If you haven't seen one before, the adult white and black, seagull-sized bird looks as though someone dipped their webbed bird feet—and only their feet—in aqua-blue paint. I read the blue feet (and blue legs actually) are the result of a voracious consumption of blue-scaled sardines, the stunning effect said to attract mates. (Elvis did sing about his blue suede shoes?) It feels as though the nonchalant Boobies are just trying to get on with their day-to-day lives while successive groups of tourists materialize to gawk at them and poke right into the middle of their intimate living quarters. (*Geez, here comes another batch of those featherless, ugly-footed creatures!*) Imagine having successive flocks of birds lasciviously peering into your bedroom!

Apparently, the word "booby" derives from the Spanish "bobo" meaning "dunce." It stems from their clumsy gait on land, lack of fear for humans and habit of laying eggs directly in plain sight, as in the middle of the footpath before us. It is startling to see wildlife so lackadaisical in our presence. What's the deal? You are supposed to fly off in mortal fear! Shoo! Shoo! But these guys clearly *expect us to move*. Extraordinary.

---

* Courtney's silently harbored reflection: *THIS is what I endured two hours of miserable agony on that boat for!!!* XX%***##ooXX%X@Xxx!

Pushing beyond the tableland, it is necessary to hike out to the rougher edges of the island to seek out the frigates. Just as we are climbing, anguishing up and through yet more hot barren volcanic rock—unquestionably the nadir of our trek—spontaneous proselytizing begins. Two of the young women we had falsely assessed to be average college kids, begin evangelizing full-throttle—in stereo. It is as if this purgatorial exorcism of a hike is to remind us of our destiny should we foolishly reject *their personal lord and savior.*

Now, my natural inclination, when subjected to aggressive preaching, is to instantly feel defensive, annoyed, and unreceptive. I don't know why this is. In my more mature years I make an attempt at tolerance, at patience when put in this position. I do appreciate the *sincerity of their motives,* their *youthful exuberance* to share what they believe to be the *one and only truth.* However, Carly is another matter. I can feel her beginning to steam (not at all hard in this climate). Of course we are supportive of any work that alleviates human suffering, but, as appreciators of cultural diversity, such a one-dimensional mindset is often detrimental to the preservation of vulnerable and valuable native cultures. The well-documented damage inflicted by such an attitude is irrefutable. (I.e., removing Native American children from their families and forcing them into boarding schools.) One would hope that in contemporary times evangelism is coupled with a large degree of respect and humility for the host country's cultural integrity, and that there is an open-mindedness toward differing philosophies—not the incessant (many would say arrogant) domination of Western thought.

Unfortunately, I do not detect a scintilla of willingness from these young women to entertain any differing viewpoints other than a strictly dogmatic, denominational-specific agenda. Yahweh or no way.

Disheartening.

"By sharing our different beliefs and unique insights, we can enrich each other, not by emulating each other's way of life, but by opening ourselves to other points of view." ~ The Dalai Lama

As we are now dealing with environmental destruction on a global scale recall the long-espoused wisdom of the Native Americans claiming the inter-connectedness of all life on Earth (as well respect for Mother Earth) that is now completely substantiated by science. The prescient environmental philosophy takes your breath away with its contemporary accuracy.

"Treat the earth well. It was not given to you by your parents, it was loaned to you by your children. We do not inherit the Earth from our Ancestors, we borrow it from our Children." *Ancient Indian Proverb*

"The first peace, which is the most important, is that which comes within the souls of people when they realize their relationship, their oneness with the universe and all its powers, and when they realize that at the center of the universe dwells the Great Spirit, and that this center is really everywhere, it is within each of us." *Black Elk*, Oglala Sioux

"When all the trees have been cut down, when all the animals have been hunted, when all the waters are polluted, when all the air is unsafe to breathe, only then will you discover you cannot eat money." *Cree Prophecy*

SOON THE AIR IS FILLED WITH LARGE, BLACK, SPLIT-TAILED FRIGATES, cascading, diving, plummeting amongst the rough lava cliffs that loom over the turbulent ocean. The spectacle is eerie and evokes a dark predatory sense not unlike a mass of vultures, but most befitting the island's desolate terrain. We soon have our first encounter with the roosting male Magnificent Frigate bird (Fregata magnificens). Nestled within the sun-baked hillside of desiccated twigs and brush, the handful of males bring to mind escaped red party balloons, blown asunder, haphazardly trapped in debris—i.e., like random balloons with birds attached to them. Beneath their long, hooked beaks, this mostly black bird possesses a bright red, inflatable "gular pouch." When expanded this several inch (five to seven?) taut protrusion is intended to attract a mate, like projecting a big red-heart valentine to the sky chicks. The flamboyant display is completely bizarre, the red protrusion a startling contrast against the dull-hued landscape. For awhile I study the loose waddle of skin hanging on the necks of the non-inflated (something I am, unfortunately, beginning to relate to with age); these guys must be on break. The lengths nature goes in order to propagate itself defies comprehension; the selected attributes seem more like the work of an *Alice in Wonderland* Mad Hatter.

Though novel to me, apparently frigates are found all along the Americas' tropical coastlines.

From here, we come upon another rest stop built to provide the only shelter from the sun. It is perched on a rocky outcrop overlooking the island's distant shoreline and expansive ocean view. A lashed-timber roof shades one paltry table and two paltry wooden benches. Gwyneth Paltrow is sitting there ... (we are crazed and hallucinating by this point). We drag ourselves beneath its shade, collapsing in the oven-like, breezeless air. I pretend to ignore Gwyneth's presence.

> Courtney sprawled out on her back, lying across the hard wood table of the rest stop. I wonder what whimsical daydreaming was floating through her head …
>
> **"I was thinking about how I could burn down that damn boat so I wouldn't have to get back on it … but, then I'd end up being stuck in this godforsaken place."**

My energy reserves depleted, I gaze lethargically at the undulating trail; it snakes downwards, at least another mile or so, towards the distant, muted shore. The entire vista appears hazy, like a mirage in shimmering heat. The rock-hard ground radiates visible heat waves back to the sky. It's oppressive, as though we are trapped inside a sealed terrarium, the half spheres of sky and water equally weighted to the other. Midway on the far trail, a group of wavering, behatted hikers inch their way along the sinuous path. Going down means coming back up again. No, I can't do it.

Most of our group opt to stay put and wait until the others return from the shore.

But it isn't much better languishing in the stagnant heat either. Hidden from view on the far side of a cliff, further down the barren trail, lie more frigate mating grounds. I weigh the bird viewing prospects against exhaustion: knowing with utmost certainty I WILL NEVER COME BACK HERE AGAIN, I feel it incumbent upon myself to somehow summon up the strength to *will myself* around that corner!

I offer my suggestion. Courtney and Carly—eyes firmly shut—FLATLY REFUSE TO BUDGE. *Geesh, it's just a thought!* I am vaguely aware of the other touristy bodies, congregated and comatose with us under the shelter. They aren't going anywhere either. Though fearful of enduring yet more harsh sun exposure, I steel myself to persevere (I make it sound like I'm summiting K2), stagger back onto and ramble down the path.

The first thing I come across, directly behind a sign that says *Stay on the Path,* is a blonde, hippie girl, off the path and inside the brush, smoking a joint all by herself. Am I hallucinating again? I try to give her space, as she

116

coolly stares off into space. Gutsy. A cheery *Hello!* from me doesn't seem in the least bit appropriate, so I quietly move on.

A bit further down the path, and then—Eureka! I find the mother lode of mate-summoning male frigates! Covering the entire hillside are protruding scarlet, blown-up gular pouches! But this time, accompanying the sight, is the beating sound of a taut drum: *rata tatatatat rata tatatatat rata tatatatat.* The male birds, heads strained backwards from their bulging, bulbous chests, are soundly beating the stretched skin with their long, overhanging beaks. Their own bodies supply a mating drum! Wow! (Some chicks always do go for the drummer!) Nature is soooooooo bizarre!

In awe, I hot foot it (literally) back to get the girls. But boy is it a hard sell! "It had better be worth it," hisses Courtney as though she's risen from the dead. Carly stumbles along, bringing up the rear.

Thank God, it is worth it.

Eventually, our mates rejoin us and it is time to head back. I have no recollection of how we did this—I guess I blocked it out. The next thing I remember is being back on that boat again.

All Aboard

Courtney is our appreciator of good food, so when we are served a brown bag lunch of dry and crusty *tuna-like* (?) sandwiches, an unnaturally bright orange, ultra-sweet, canned fruit drink and some *strange brand* crackers, she is not a happy camper. "Just the opposite of what you'd ever want on a super hot day," rejects Courtney. Her stomach still unsteady, she shoves all her rations aside. Insult upon injury. Carly and I fall upon her crackers. I try to chew on one of the sandwiches, but it proves to be too much effort in the oppressive heat.

Bobbing along, it is now time for the snorkeling part of our adventure. We troll along the shoreline for about five minutes until we come upon the advertised, promised "secluded island cove." Yes, it is secluded, but it is also filled with other major tourist boats. Oh well.

I am determined to live life to the fullest, go for the gusto, i.e., actually get in the water! (Remember we are not water people.) Plus—and this weighs heavily on my decision—the thought of languishing for two more hours as my sweaty, filthy self is too much to bear. To the look of amazement (which quickly turns to amusement) from my gutless daughters, I alone (among the three of us) decide to suit up and snorkel. They grab their cameras to capture the momentous occasion.

Now, the process of suiting up is an adventure in itself. The only place to change is a below-deck privy about the size of Saddam Hussein's spider hole. Dropping down some narrow stairs, I face a tiny door. Taking a deep breath, I pitch myself forward and latch myself into complete darkness (all power is off on the anchored vessel). Extraordinarily claustrophobic! I hold my breath as I struggle not to touch or brush against anything icky. Finding no place to put discarded clothes, I hang on to them while fumbling with buttons and zippers and performing a one-legged balancing act, careful to remove and replace each shoe before the other hits the ground (I don't want to step on anything icky either.)

After what seems like an eternity of awkward finagling, I finally burst out the door, gasping for fresh air.

118

Back up on deck I am given a yellow goggle/snorkel set, orange life vest and green flippers. Next I am to put a dripping, antiseptic-wet, rubber mouthpiece in my mouth pulled straight from a sloshing bucket of twelve others! *Ewwwwwwww*, I am so hoping they have sterilized it thoroughly!!!' Equipped thusly, I am met with peals of laughter from my indelicate progeny. *What?* [See photo for easy explanation]

Now, my anticipatory dread of cold shocking water nearly paralyzes me. I cannot describe with adequate revulsion how much I hate this sensation; it is the sole reason I rarely go swimming. Flopping in my flippers to the edge of the boat I sit down, brace myself, grab my goggles and lean backwards into the ocean water (ála Lloyd Bridges/Flipper).

Aaaaagggggghhhhh! Cringing, skin-prickling, bucket of ice down the back torment! I HATE IT SOOOOOOOOOOOOOOOOOOOO MUCH!!!

And then it's over; I suffer no more. Paddle, paddle. I'm still alive.

(Drat! I can see that Marshmallowmom from Jersey— my middle-aged nemesis—jumping in right after me!)

My world consists now of nothing but pronounced breathing: wheeze-gurgle, in and out, wheeze-gurgle, in and out (there's some water trapped in my snorkel hence the gurgle). All I can think about is Dustin Hoffman's swimming pool scene in *The Graduate*—a deadened water-silence all but for my solitary breathing. *Okay, now don't swallow any water Dorothy* (my thoughts are really loud too). Blowing out I try to expel the trapped water but fail. The gurgling persists. Oh well. Through the distorted lens of goggles and water, I vaguely make out the girls pointing and laughing at me. Wheeze-gurgle-gasp. My arms extended straight out, paddling in squares, left, right, right left, left right left. They are laughing a lot! I will move away from them and their petty cruelties. Flip flip, KERPLUNK splash. (I do like that solid *kerplunk!* sound made from my boldly-thrashing flippers.)

---

*   3/1/11 Looking up information on the Internet I came across one fellow's story about this very same boat tour. I was horrified to read that within 24 hours his mouth exploded in sores exactly where the snorkel mouthpiece had been. According to his account, the infection was incurable. I never know when I'm being neurotic or sensible (making my life very difficult indeed).

Beyond the maze of boats, I spot an overhanging cliff. I resolve to swim to it and back for a reasonably adequate venture. Wheeze-gurgle-kerplunk-splash. The underwater view is not like a spectacular Hawaiian-burst-of-color[*] but a few schools of colorful fish do whisk by me, cutting through the murky green water. In record time, I make it to the overhanging cliff. Okay, I see three really big fish, now I can go back. Turning around to face my return journey, I suddenly realize … ***OMG! All the tourist boats look alike!*** PANIC! I don't know which one is mine! ***WHY DIDN'T I STUDY IT MORE BEFORE I LEFT!!!?***

Was it blue or white or aqua? Could it have already left without me? Surely the girls would've noticed I hadn't returned! ("Do ta do ta doo … Courtney, did we leave anything behind … something just doesn't seem right," as Carly examines her cuticles and files her nails on the speeding-away boat. "Oh well, it'll probably come to us later.")

Or another imagined scenario: The girls are pleading: "Please Señor Boat Captain, you cannot just leave our mother out there!" El Capitan: "I am sorry but we have a very strict schedule to maintain. Perhaps another boat will spot her dogpaddling under the full moon tonight. Full speed ahead!"

Like a confused pinball I ricochet off each boat. Are you my boat? Are you my boat? No! Ahhhhhh! Wheeze-gurgle-slosh. No! Ahhhhhh! Wheeze-gurgle-slosh. It has to be here somewhere!!!

Six or eight boats later I chance upon my vessel … that I now notice is named *La Esperanza* (The Hope). I am greatly relieved. Carly expresses that she was "beginning to feel concern over my prolonged absence." Courtney chirps in, "I wasn't."

---

[*] Once upon a time, on a snorkeling escapade off a Maui catamaran, we were each issued an underwater camera as part of the tour. Besides the glorious display of fantastically colored fish, I could not believe my luck that a large jelly fish was swiftly swimming toward me! I excitedly snapped photo after photo as it came near. Wow, this was so cool … until it came near enough that I realized … I had taken several photos of … a plastic bag.

RETURN VOYAGE: More of the same (second verse, same as the first ... a little bit greener and a whole lot worse).

It turns overcast and a gray sea reflects a gray sky as we look for gray whales. The boat pauses several times—the idling engine wafts nauseating fumes over the deck—bobbing up and down, and up and down, on rolls and rolls of rolling waves. Everyone's trying to ignore Courtney's retching wretchedness, positioning themselves as far away from her as possible on the far perimeters of the boat. The tour directors try their best to come up with some whales while balancing the extent of agony Courtney can endure. Eventually, they have to give it up (I suspect a little earlier than normal).

Blessedly landing on shore, we are once again besieged by children, this time carrying old, quart-sized glass pop bottles filled with murky water (?); Carly explains they are hoping to wash the sand off our feet for money. Not a bad idea, though I have no money on me.

Courtney's assessment of her "Diablo Island" day:

Finally stepping on *terra firma* and regaining some degree of stability, an outburst of resentment pours forth: "I see how it is! I'm going to paint some bird's feet blue and tape a red balloon to its neck and charge sixty bucks just to see it! Then I'll point out over the ocean and say, 'Oh look, it's a whale, no, it's a wave! That'll be another fifty bucks!'"

And this is where Roberto picks up and deposits his soiled and bedraggled gringas back at the hotel, looking as though we had been hog-tied and dragged behind a horse for several low-tide miles.

Nirvana at Night

I think it was the fevered delirium of the day, the flip-side of suffering and torment that produces the euphoric happiness that follows. For whatever reason, the dopamine is flowing this evening as we walk the city streets. Musicians play flutes and congas in the small central cobblestone plaza, residents languidly posture on balconies above and on adobe stoops below, enjoying the wafting music suspended on the soft evening breezes. The setting is so idyllic I nearly expect all the characters, on some hidden cue, to break into a song from a Broadway musical!

At this very moment, the oddest sensation sweeps over me, a *recognition*, a feeling *that I belong here.* Yeah, right! I also recognize the absurdity of such a déjà vu moment, but it is so strong ... and pleasurable! Who knows, perhaps the tropical warmth taps into the primal origin of our being, that our cellular selves recognize and blissfully absorb the warm temperature in which we were meant to live. (The same temperature we keep our thermostats up north.)

We return to the previous night's Colombian café to right a dreadful wrong: this time I order the kebob with Courtney and Carly gets the french fries. It is great; we are happy. As usual, even during dinner time I want to rush around, take in as much as possible, send out e-mails in an Internet café just across the plaza—all while waiting for dinner to arrive. This drives Courtney crazy and she interjects some sense: "Why can't we just lie on the beach hammocks tonight?" *Forget the alluring shops, the unexplored side streets, and ... just ... hang?* I'm deliberating. With many misgivings, I acquiesce, and drag myself behind them toward the beach bars. "Fine, I'll try it."

It proves to be one of the best decisions ever.

The modest, thatched-roof and bamboo cane bars on the beach turn out to be heavenly. Each bar displays exotic, glowing lanterns in distinctive hourglass designs of all sizes (made of dyed, stretched goat skin I believe)—some as tall as six feet emanate warm oranges and purples. (I'd love to take one home, but I'd have to carry it everywhere.) All the lanterns and beach campfires are fueled by smoke-free natural gas. Each club has its own modest dance floor (say 20' by 20') surrounded by open air speakers.

The collision of sound is the only way to distinguish where one bar stops and the other begins. But the best part of the whole set-up is that these are *hammock bars!** So while sipping on the beverage of choice you are amongst a rainbow grouping of hammocks, swaying beneath an open-air thatched-roof, the warm breezes and sound of the ocean mingling with music. Talk about nirvana. Looking down the beach all you can see in the darkness is the colorful continuation of glowing orange lanterns and golden beach fires, all with their own encircled hammock lounges. It is very, very magical.

The girls and I rock in our hammocks and sip our smoothies, laughing and happy together. Finally, I am appreciating the simple pleasure of *just hanging.* (Dang, that Courtney is right!)

Before we leave, I linger to watch a handful of people blissfully dancing away on a tiny wooden dance floor, swaying to the Ambrosia song, *"That's how much I feel for you baby ..."*

Ahhhhhhh, so romantic, what a beautiful evening! †

---

* What a concept! Why can't I think of these things? And how to replicate this glorious feeling back home ... but I'd need an ocean as a backdrop!

† The only fly in the ointment: As I was writing my e-mails in the Internet café that night, an Australian woman pulled me over, *gushing* over her whale footage she had shot that day on *her* boat tour (of a breaching whale no less), eager to share with me her fabulous luck. I accidentally leaned on the "permanently delete" button (twice) as I directed her attention to a UFO landing in the plaza.

Hike from Hell
No Parrots, No Monkeys

Puerto López   *Aug. 6 e-mail*

Well, we are having quite the adventure. I think I love South America because it is still a wild, nitty-gritty place. Most people have been incredibly nice. My favorite place has been the Agua Blanca indigenous community with thatched roof dwellings, pigs, goats, etc. They had an actual archeological dig in situ showing remains of a pre-Columbian civilization. I loved that but their little museum had several pickled, poisonous snakes!

We feel like queens being driven around in our motocab everywhere by Roberto. He is so kind and said his heart will be very sad when we leave. He beeps his roadrunner-sounding-like horn at everyone in town (he must have lots of friends). We are returning to Agua Blanca today for an adventurous hike up to the cloud forest!

Now here's what happens that day: Our group hike should have been called:

"Dry Gulch Diaspora"

Setting the scene: The first mistake, our second day in Puerto López:

Bright and early, Carly and I are the first to meet at our hotel's outdoor breakfast table, poolside. Here our nice, but *oh so slooowwww,* waiter metes out our morning ration of caffeine—a tiny cup consisting of 3/4 milk and 1/4 weak Nescafé. I soon learn to skip the milk and order extra cups for invisible friends. It is an excruciatingly slow process for Seattle-affected super consumers. More often than not—annoyed by my pained expression and wonton covetousness—Carly relinquishes her portion to me, just to wipe the glum look off my face AND to smugly establish herself as superior when it comes to developing-world adaptation. I've no shame; I'll take it! (*Bluck! She already added five teaspoons of sugar!!!*) After the coffee, we're served the hotel's complimentary breakfast of beaten eggs, jelly and a meager supply of bread. (We couldn't face those heavily buttered eggs by the third day. And we couldn't get more bread either.)

Carly and I discuss our preparations for the next day's dry-jungle jaunt up to the cloud forest. Informed that it is *at least* a four-hour trek— and though we are used to physical exertion—I weigh this with much gravitas, thinking this is a pretty significant endeavor in light of the fact that we are on the equator. Unspoken between us is the reservation about Courtney's participation, still reeling from the previous day's disastrous boat ride. (She now vilely refers to *Isla de la Plata* as "Diablo Island.") We are both harboring the unspoken wish that she will just take the day off and read poolside rather than risk her potent wrath should things go wrong again.

A surly Courtney soon joins us. We inform her of our plans. Her eyes narrow in distrust and deliberation as she weighs her options. She's indecisive and wary. I mistakenly offer up this kernel of wisdom, "Well, I would hate for you to miss out on a unique opportunity if it turns out wonderful." (A National Geographic image of a misty, sun-streaked tropical forest, fluttering butterflies and the mystical hooting of wild creatures danced in my head.) This nudges her into the affirmative column and Carly shoots me a look of incredulity. *Mother! You moron! She'll make our lives a living hell if it turns out badly!* (I sense this entire reproach just from her panic-stricken eyes.)

Once Court apprehensively acquiesces to go, she threatens us through clenched teeth:

"I BETTER SEE A MONKEY."

Mistake number two: We need to determine if we should arrange to rent horses or walk the long trek. We weigh this carefully and I'm thinking *I would rather be miserably hot on a horse than miserably hot on foot* (if it comes to that). So we throw away sixty-dollars on horses we end up sending back.

THE DAY BEGINS overcast, misty and threatening rain. Roberto arrives early in his motocab and suggests we take our raincoats along, "just in case." So we retrieve them from our room and stuff them all into one backpack. (*Who cares? We'll be on horses anyway!*) Skirting Puerto López, we continue north along the coastal highway for our return trip to the charming little settlement of Agua Blanca. Once there, we join a group of about ten people lurking about, waiting for the tour to begin. We are the only ones to have rented horses.

Little did I know at the time, it would be over six grueling hours before I would ever see this comforting little hamlet again.'

HORSE SADDLE-UP FIASCO I don't know who has more fear in their eyes: us, the horses, or the horse handlers. We attempt to mount the gargantuan, foreign beasts while the local *indígena* guys hold the reigns steady. With only one tennis-shoed foot in the stirrups, we three get caught up in a synchronized whirlwind of confusion. The reign-holders dare not let go as they spin in circles along with us. We look like a choreographed version of Dancing with the Mares.

Once situated atop the horse, my dangling other foot finally finds the opposite stirrup. Now there's the giddy thrill and rush of an adventure at the start! Wow, look at us! Riding horses in the jungles of Ecuador!

This doesn't last long.

Carly is the first to embark on the very dusty trail, followed by me, and then Courtney. I quickly lose sight of Carly in the dry, treed foliage as she disappears around a bend. Before long the jungle resounds with high-pitched screaming. Carly's horse has taken off in a mad dash, bounding off the trail and through the brambles. It seems he caught the whiff of his amour ♥ pasturing in an off-trail banana grove (a recurring problem we are later told). Stopped only by a barbed-wire fence, his horse face hanging over the other side, Romeo refuses to budge from his besotted position.

---

* San Sebastián Hike: round trip 20 km (about 12 and a half miles); Cloud Forest 600 meters up (about 2000 ft.) from Agua Blanca's 65 meters (213 ft. elevation); from tropical dry forest to tropical moist forest.

And Carly can't find reverse. "Heeeelllllp, heeeeelllllllp!" she shrieks from the bramble bush.

Peering over my shoulder, I look back to see a tremulous and faltering Courtney. Three people are trying to keep her from sliding off her mount. Her emaciated-looking horse lists from side to side and attempts to meander off course whenever he can. "MOM, there is something REALLY WRONG with this horse!" she pleads helplessly

And I am experiencing my own version of horse-terror. (S)he is very adept at maneuvering me under any low-hanging branch in attempts to scrape me off its back. I'm clutching my saddle and grasping the horn in a very low crouch each time a termite-infested branch nearly swipes me across the face and off my mount. But worse than this, from my high altitude perch I detect an unsure-footedness of my horse; it stumbles precariously on a dangerously steep, rocky escarpment. I have visions of us plunging to our deaths together—horse and rider rolling over and over and over again—full of *termitos*.

It does not take long at all before we are all in a flux of confusion. I issue an order to dismount, regroup and reassess the situation.

Safely on the ground, we huddle in group conference as everyone impatiently waits for us to make a decision; it's a foot-and-finger-tapping moment. As the guys hold the horses steady, the pros and cons are weighed: we'll lose our money ... or our lives. It's also disconcerting to have the rest of the group walk behind us (perched on our High Horses so to speak), an elevated status that feels as though we're some kind of pampered gringas. Furthermore, I am humbled by an older couple tackling it on foot. I am shamed; if they can do it surely we can! (I didn't realize at the time that they were in it only for the short term—turning around at a soon-to-be-reached, prearranged spot.)

All this influences my decision to jettison the horses. All death scenarios considered, (heatstroke on the ground or horse-death by air) it seems we would be *more likely to survive* on foot. So, the horses go back.

Well, EVERYONE ELSE on this tour brought only a water bottle and bug spray to carry. We brought a whole pack of non-essential stuff (raincoats, guidebooks, floral displays, formal outdoor chinaware, etc.) all stuffed into one backpack. Carly is the first to sling it over her shoulders. Soon the more elderly folks turn around at milepost one and the group headed to the cloud forest is reduced to seven. Besides us, there is a 27-year-old, athletic looking Brazilian guy, dressed in bright yellow sports attire, and two early twenties Spanish girls, wearing jeans and t-shirts, all led by our late thirtyish *indígena* guide, who is dressed in polo shirt and khaki slacks and carries a machete.

As advised (even by the locals), we are covered from head to toe in protective clothing so as not to get sunburned or become gringa-flavored sushi for untold foreign *insectos*. We begin our foot trek up to the cloud forest, and I do mean UP. The path ascends relentlessly. *Good God*, I keep thinking after we slog to numerous crests, *we can't still be going up*. And yet each incline is followed by another and another and another. I peer over my shoulder to see how the others in our group are doing: They appear to me unhappy, sweating and struggling too.

This is the most I have ever perspired in my entire life—collectively. Soon Carly and I (Courtney escaped the over-active sweat gene) look like we took our clothes straight out of the washing machine—no spin cycle. I am not in the least bit exaggerating. Once we hit a fairly level spot, Carly has had it carrying the backpack, and it is my turn to take up the load. (Most of the items in the pack are ours, and we are perpetually fearful of Courtney.)

On a more positive note, for the very first time ever I am able to thoroughly use my high-end sporting goods apparel (i.e., my multi-vented, UPF sun block treated shirt $$$) to the nth degree. Previously, my very expensive shirt had only experienced a less than 6.5 mile hiking excursion on (what now seem) pristine pathways in mostly agreeable weather. I always felt kind of guilty about that. No more. One by one all the mysteries dissipated for each and every functional design: every Velcro flap, zippered vent, mesh-lining purpose become perfectly clear. *So that's what that's for* I think as I realize how the mesh behind the three desperately-needed air circulating vents stops bugs; that the once mysterious Velcro on my collar fastens to an upright position, protecting against both sun and insects; that the "wick away perspiration" fabric keeps my shirt from pasting to me like a molded paper mâché project gone bad. *Geesh*, they must've tested and designed this thing specifically for Parque Nacional Machalilla San Sebastián Forest!

Finally, I am getting my money's worth.

Before long my long pants are so saturated in sweat I can no longer tolerate the heavy drag on my body. After about the seventh hill, it becomes unbearable. I hope that layer of DEET insect repellent does its job. I unzip and remove the bottom part of my pant legs. Carly is stripping too, all the way down to a tank top and shorts ("I don't care! I can't take it anymore!" she wails.) She flings off her protective clothing. Courtney, on the other hand, blessed with the sweet blood of her father and his propensity to attract any hungry insect within a five mile radius, is besieged by bugs. Like nothing I've ever seen before. SCREECH!!! SCREECH!!! "MOTHER!!!" I run to her side to find her pant legs indistinguishable beneath a layer of weird insects. "What are they, what are they?" she dances around. "Get them off!" Hearing the clamor, our guide backtracks and, assessing the situation, calmly takes his machete and shaves off the thick insect layer from her pants. Matter settled. Unfortunately, we have to stop for several repeat performances (Carly and I, both now in shorts, have no problem whatsoever.) At one point, two in our group take pity on her distress and share their precious bug spray by saturating the fabric of both pant legs. Unbelievably, even this does not solve the problem.

I try to inject some levity into the situation by merrily singing, "Oooooh, there ain't no bugs, there ain't no bugs, no, there ain't no bugs on me, there might be bugs on some of your mugs, but there ain't no bugs on me," to which Courtney shoots poison-dart looks my way. I determine it is in my best interests to cease and desist.

Finally, reaching some kind of plateau, we pause and pull out our one ... shared ... water bottle. Courtney eyes this with incredulity. "You mean that's the only water you brought? WE'RE GOING TO GET DEHYDRATED!!!" she throws her head back in wailing dismay, voice bouncing off the monkey-less tree branches.

But wait! Our leader thinks he may hear a monkey hoot. Could this wretched hike be saved by an exotic animal sighting? Courtney re-sheathes her knife. We all listen attentively. Nope. False alarm. Apparently the phantom monkey moved on. Nothing whatsoever to redeem us.

About a half hour later, I see the group is huddling around a wild animal of sorts. Halleluiah! Finally a reason to be on this hike! I rush up to see what is causing the commotion, only to find ... only to find ..... they are looking at .... a squirrel. Albeit a squirrel with a long tail but IT'S STILL A SQUIRREL! I could see this in any city park at home!!!! Agggghhhhh!

Crestfallen, we continue on our slog.'

---

* My mind wandered to every movie I'd ever seen about agonizing jungle ventures gone awry (I was suffering so much I felt completely justified in this indulgence); soiled, tight kerchief around the neck, perspiration-soaked t-shirt, plotting as to who is the weakest and flailing among us, the first to be sacrificed, their precious water supply divvied up ... *hey, that's probably me!*

Bonded in Wretchedness

Every once in a while Carly pauses to *selectively* frame aesthetic, exotic-looking photos. Courtney, on the other hand, turns her back and shoots at the wasteland, "So I can remember just how ugly this is," she flatly states. (And to expose us as bare-faced liars in any attempt to portray this as a worthwhile experience to family and friends back home.)

Trudging, anguishing, along, I raise my head in a haze of despondence to notice some trees in the distance wavering about with white blobs all over them. I try to distinguish just what it is: it can't be flowering trees because that would be fragile and lovely. It is only later that I realize it was the silk-cotton pods of the noteworthy kapok tree.*

Now well into our fifth hellish hour, we're endlessly traversing through a narrow, dried-up creek bed, engulfed by hard dirt and rock embankments, scattered rocks underfoot twisting our ankles. (It is here I spot one vivid blue butterfly instantaneously flit away, my only exotic wildlife sighting.) Sporadically, in response to our feeble inquiries as to when this nightmare would end, our guide keeps repeating *"cerquita cerquita"* (meaning really close or only a few more minutes) to keep us hanging on. LIES LIES LIES! The few minutes easily turn into ninety!†

It is at this point Courtney falls down in the dry tropical forest—with plenty of ears to hear it.

I am some distance behind, immersed in my own miasma of misery, when I hear what sounds like an animal crashing through the brush. *What the hell was that? Oooooooh Noooooooooooo! Courtney fell down!* Terror grips my heart. Racing to her side, extending a helping hand, I see she is grinning ... a creepy grin of delirium. She had fallen face forward, rolled onto her

---

*   Not being any kind of a seamstress I had no idea *kapok* is a familiar material used as an alternative to down for insulation and padding in things like pillows and life preservers; before the synthetic version came out, its buoyant, water-repellent qualities were invaluable as life vest material during the world wars

†   The thought occurred separately and regularly to both Carly and I that had we persuaded Courtney to stay behind that day and read poolside *we would have been sooooo grateful she hadn't come along!*

back, and has chosen to *stay down* and rest for awhile, strewn among the dry-bed rocks cradling her form. When she refuses to get up, Carly and I become alarmed—scared that once she does get to her feet she will transmogrify into a demonic-force shape-shifter, grab the guide's machete and make short work out of both of us—all while suspended in midair: We become instant *carne blanca!* (white meat) for all the hovering vultures! (These menacing-looking predators are everywhere and *so apropos* to the environment.) Thankfully, our guide is a potential credible witness. He is standing right there. She has to behave.

Meanwhile, the three other hikers in our group have fallen further and further behind. At this point, we haven't seen them for quite some time. Earlier on our guide would stop and patiently wait for them to catch up, but now he seems to just shrug it off and give up, seemingly with a *más o menos* (more or less), easy come, easy go, attitude. There are so many confusing forks in the trail I can't imagine why he isn't more concerned? Does he know something I don't? Every once in a while, peering back over my shoulder, I would catch glimpses of the bright yellow sports attire of the Brazilian guy—but the last sighting of him was oh-so long ago (he kept doubling back to help the two young Spanish women who were even further behind). I can't understand the complacency of our leader by their absence? Are we beyond caring? Is our sense of decency, our basic bond, our belief in the intrinsic value of all human life in question?

Oh well.

Oh, Lord, I cannot adequately convey the depth of our misery. And there is the excruciating mental torture of so many false positives! Sighting a few thatched roofs or some kind of clearing we'd be thinking *Thank God it is finally over!* We have inarguably *endured* and *suffered* far beyond our normal capacity! *But no*, to our utter disbelief again and again and again the dismal trail just keeps writhing forward and onward. One barren road even had the audacity to lead up though we are supposed to be going down! How much more can we take!!?

From an elevated position, I glance back at Carly and her exposed white-tone legs, as she languishes up and through the umpteenth dry gulch;

stamina so severely tested, so utterly depleted that giving expression to torment is not an option. Courtney is around a bend pulling up the rear, still attired from head to foot in all her heavy protective clothing. Carly and I keep passing the backpack back and forth between us.

All of us are in non-speaking survival mode as we stagger as solos across the terrain.

As this *diaspora of turistas* struggles along, a little girl, on the base of a hillock above, waves to us from a bamboo cane hut while her mother hangs laundry. I can't imagine how deranged and haggard we look. What can they make of us? (I'll guess *loco*.) We then walk through a tiny hamlet, passing beneath a large communal volleyball net, beautifully made with its wooden posts blending into the environment. Very attractive, had I enough energy to care.

"How much further???" "*Cerquita, cerquita.*"

By the time we walk into the Agua Blanca settlement—nearly seven grueling hours after starting—we appear as dazed zombies. Even dragging ourselves across the parking lot over to the restaurant takes more painstaking effort.

As the sole patrons, we sit down. Our pale, blank faces and fixated-stares (no energy to blink) face one another across the wooden table.

So utterly fatigued, even resting isn't restful.

It is here Courtney finally breaks. Exploding, out floods a torrent:

"What's wrong with you two!!!? Why do you always have to be doing something!!!?" And continuing in sputtering frustration, "Why can't we ever just sit down ... AND ... AND ... AND ... SIT?!!!" (Is that considered an activity? I ponder.)

Looking back, this seems the zenith of our entire journey, the point from which everything began to glide downhill in a smoother momentum. Kind of like an unintentional boot camp, Courtney's residual teenage walls and defenses came tumbling down: We inadvertently bonded through a shared hell.

We order cold Cokes and water all around. The most appreciated, best tasting Coke on earth. Our prepaid, prearranged luncheon courses begin arriving one by one: hot corn and shrimp chowder soup, fried banana chips, fried potatoes, fried corn and deep-fried battered fish. Under other circumstances, wonderful. Under ours, not. All we want, can tolerate, are fluids; the last thing our bodies crave are heavy fried foods. We only nibble at our $17 meals and leave most of it behind.

Roberto to the Rescue Back in our chariot, streaming away downhill, the wind in our hair, we feel a rush of freedom, of intense relief! Finally! *Wheeeeeeeeee! We're alive and free and released from hell!* But then it suddenly occurs to us: after all this time we still haven't seen anything of our lost trio of comrades? Our exhilaration momentarily suspends in midair. Then, in a shameful fit of black humor, we all burst into laughter at the thought of them still bumbling about the hinterlands, still trying to make their way back. (And truly, they were in *no real danger.*) I'm not sure why this would strike us as so cruelly funny; for that answer I would have to plumb the depths of human nature.'

But, were you near in that dry-jungle forest, a trilling cascade of maniacal laughter *"ha ha ha ha ha ha ha ha"* could be heard careening down the hillside of *Parque Nacional Machalilla Agua Blanca* that one fateful day in August 2009. We were bonding again.

Free at last, free at last, God almighty, free at last!

---

*   There's even a German name for this human propensity: *Schadenfreude,* that is, pleasure from the misfortune of others. (Interesting the name "Freud" is in there ... wonder what he would make of this.) Being as how the trio was young and physically fit and in no *real peril,* if only miserable, someone could easily find them—if only they cared to look!

Back at the hotel Courtney and I engage in a much-deserved dip in the pool. In due time, exhibiting extraordinary valor, I ascend the pool's waterfall slide to impress Courtney and show her what a fun, good sport I can still be at fifty-six. Courtney hesitantly watches and is duly impressed as I plunge my cringing, water-shocked body into the water. I pretend to enjoy it. Also, above and beyond any sense of decency, I have agreed to wear the cheap yellow polyester swim suit (the one we had so hastily bought before our whale-less whale tour) generously giving Courtney the more comfortable red one (mine). The new suit presents me with *the challenge* to adequately cover either my bottom or top—not both.

Oh well, no one knows me and they'll get over it (I think). I make a meek and failed attempt to live fearlessly.

We have the pool all to ourselves, cavorting and frolicking about, when *who pops out of nowhere to join us* but MY MIDDLE-AGED NEMESIS AND HER DAUGHTER!!! With considerable aplomb she proceeds to careen up and down the slide multiple times, like it's second nature! Ugh! Is there no justice! Is there nothing I can do that's remarkable for my age!!?

She continued to shamelessly display herself as an incredibly good-natured spirit and all around good sport.

Saying goodbye to Roberto that evening is very sad. It is our final day and it is time to go. He holds his hand over his heart, eyes softening, conveying sincerity, and says, *"Las voy a extrañar"* (I will miss you). We take several last pictures together and thank him profusely for being our king, our wonderful companion, and our cohort in adventure. Once we return home, we send him the farewell pictures along with a thank you card. We hope he got them.

Otavalo

Market vendor (note characteristic draped necklace and embroidered blouse)

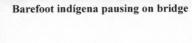

Barefoot indígena pausing on bridge

Otavaleña using *manta* (carrying wrap)

137

In neighborhood along railroad tracks (not an indigene)

Basically says "Casa for sale." Unique roof top gardening space!

Courtney showing extreme exhilaration exploring the barrios (with me).

138

Moto Cab—Roberto (rt. back) throws arms up in surrender to crazy gringas

Roberto, our wonderful driver, in front of Puerto López Bay.

One of many similar homes in Agua Blanca.

Agua Blanca's sulfur pond

Isla de Plata's Fearless Fowl: Blue-footed boobies and chicks blocking our way on the trail.

"I double-dog dare them to pass through *these* buff tail feathers."

Me ready to snorkel (planning to submit to the *Sports Illustrated* swimsuit edition)

Los Frailes Beach

Cuenca

Laundry Day—headed to
Tomebamba River

Typical caged
grocery store

Hostile in Hostal. "*I hate you.*" "*I hate you too.*" Smile for the photo girls!
(hostal is a small hotel)

Pampamesa Feast

Cañari breakfast

**Drop spindle lesson with
llama wool**

The Photographers

143

Overview & Major Digression

An Outsider's View by a Passing-Through Traveler

What I love about Latin America is the underlying vibrancy of *life*—the moving, colorful energy at every level, the straight shots of human creativity. There is no filter or plastic wrap between the grit and vitality of daily human existence.

The flow of **passion.** Sensuous energy. There's nothing uptight in this cultural experience (except me). Even political paintings splashed across state buildings throb with intense emotion: vibrant reds, yellows and purples (none of that staid government stuff). Everywhere there is unabashed human expression—including the graffiti. Aspects of the predominant mestizo population translate into a heavy Spanish influence of flowery language, flourishing romance and earthy love of food.

Color. In the bustling, prospering markets everyday life seems permeated with vivid artistry (at least in the towns we encounter on the Gringo Route); not in addition to, or created as a separate entity from, but naturally manifesting itself throughout. (You could say the antithesis of a strip mall.) For example, while walking amid the human din of Otavalo's city core, I raised my eyes to notice every lamp post individually adorned by expert metallurgy and glistening, cascading stained-glass. Such creative *personal* energy emits a strong positive charge; the drabness and stultifying affect of mass production (as in *Made in China*) delightfully absent. Of course, I'm aware a good deal is staged for the sake of tourism, but that does not diminish the astonishing, underlying skill.

From my northern-latitude perspective, many aspects of life here seem suffused with works highlighting and celebrating the beauty, bounty and power of the Sun, be it through multicolored weaves, shimmering stained glass, or fresh market produce plucked straight from the fields, bursting with wild vitality. The sun is thought the fount of natural abundance. Believe me, in chilly Andean altitudes, when the sun does warm you, it is easy to feel as though a *blissful grace* has been lavished upon you, filtering down from the heavens, bequeathed by a benevolent and powerful Sun-god. (It is also easy to imagine the desire to curry favor with this life-giving force through precious, sacrificial offerings.) After a long chilly morning,

147

it is a luscious feeling—like that of warming cold stones, of a lazing cat
basking in the sun of a winter window … ahhhhh.

The **indigenous cultures** are fascinating. The manner of dress is beyond
bizarre at first sight (i.e., a novelty with which my brain is utterly unfamiliar).
I often feel as though I have been transported by time capsule into a
completely alien world. The native cultures are the quintessence of *exotic*.
Take the hand-woven textiles and traditional dress alone: the intricately
woven materials, culled straight from nature's source, be it animal (llama)
or plant based (cotton), each thread and stitch rife with symbolism and
tradition, layers of inherited consciousness unbroken through centuries.
(Imagine if your family and friends created and wore hand-made, exquisitely
woven clothing, plus splendid accessories, according to ancestral heritage.)
The incorporation of European fashion—such as fedora or bowler hats—
to traditional costume makes for a mind-scrambling ensemble. Extreme
cognitive dissonance. (On the flip side, I am reminded of a piece I read
where, during a public festival, the Bolivian locals parody the uniformity of
tourists: men hopping around with cameras in hand, relentlessly snapping
photos and clad in khaki shorts, baseball cap, and backpack. Funny.)

And there are the multiple layers of spiritual beliefs, of innumerable sacred
sites and objects (*huacas*), of mountain spirits (*apus*), shamanism and all the
magical thinking involved; a belief system in which my Western-formed
consciousness is incapable of truly comprehending. (At least not without
the assistance of a culturally-sanctioned hallucinogen. See *Ayahuasca*.)

"Beneath the tranquil veneer of daily life, there lurks an underworld
of sorcery and superstition. The entire Latin continent is founded on a
bedrock of magical belief." [8] (Tahir Shah)

All the **unpredictability**! (This can be good and bad.) You are continually
open to chance. Cars break down;' riders dangle off every part of moving
vehicles; barterers angle for prices; marketers seduce with flowers; food

---

*   Not that I want my car to break down, but we Westerners tend to be so *insulated*.
I recall the most delightful experience when I was working with an adult ESL program
in Yakima. Upon returning from a field trip in which I was driving a dilapidated
college-owned van, we stalled on a busy overpass. My group of adult Latino students
instantly jumped out of our semi-bus— like it was second nature—and cheerfully

aromas sizzle and entice; and the palpable force of **music** and **dance** (and I would suppose sex, virility and fertility, but my white Anglo-Christian upbringing prevents my even mentioning this) pulsates just beneath the skin of it all. It comes at you from every direction; you must stay on your toes; YOU FEEL ALIVE.

The packed calendar of **festivals** and events, of religious observance or political commemoration is crazy (and magnificent!)—it seems as though a preponderance of Latin American communities are in a *near continuous state* of preparation for, enactment of, or mopping up after, some kind of elaborate, color-splashed production that can last for days or even a month. Long weekends are the rule for accommodating such an extensive list.

A *Sample* of Ecuadorian Holidays:

December 28-31 Year's End Celebrations. Starting with the Day of the Innocents, the entire nation symbolically prepares to enter a new year by burning human figurines in the streets as Quiteños (Quito residents) end a nearly month-long party. *A nearly month-long party?*

February 12 Anniversary of the Discovery of the Amazon River (*Can I do that for our Yakima River?*)

March and/or April Carnaval celebrated just before Lent. Carnaval is the ultimate party in the Catholic Nations of Latin America. The Ecuadorians use Carnaval to wear out their carnal desires before Lent. (*I don't remember having had that opportunity in my Catholic upbringing? What happens if they won't wear out?*) Water fights, lavish fruit and flower parades included.

Easter and Holy Week (*Semana Santa*) When traditional religious processions give way to **marathon feasts**.

June Saints Peter, Paul, and John (separately, of course) There is much outdoor processional display of elevated saint statues and all the pomp and circumstance that goes with it.

---

pushed me nearly a mile to a gas station. I was so touched by the air of jovial camaraderie in my time of need.

Dorothy E. Groszhans

June 21 Inti Raymi, the Sun-god solstice celebration. For **an entire week** the local men dress up in a variety of costumes and dance constantly, moving from house to house. (*Perhaps this summer I can persuade my husband to dress up and dance house to house in an attempt to engage our neighbors in a solstice celebration?*) There are bullfights in the plaza and regattas on Lago (Lake) San Pablo. In Otavalo, indigenous families have costume parties, that at times spill over into the streets. The Inti Raymi and Yamor festival display a combination of indigenous cosmic vision and Roman Catholicism.

July 24 Celebrating the liberator of Latin America from Spain. Get this name (true): **Simón José Antonio de la Santísima Trinidad Bolívar y Palacios Ponte y Blanco** commonly known as **Simón Bolívar.** (*I'm glad he wasn't in my ESL class "... now what is your last name? You have to pick one Sir! Please re-sheathe that weapon! I will not be intimidated, nor to compromise the integrity of my alphabetically organized files!" Imagine the fatigue of cheering for him in a sporting match.*)

September Yamor (corn beverage), Otavalo's indígenas thank Mother Earth for the maize harvest at the same time the mestizo culture pays tribute to the Nina Maria, patron Virgin of Otavalo. Maize, the symbol of fertility—vital to indigenas cosmic view—is honored just before the autumn equinox. (*Wait a minute ... the indígenas are celebrating fertility at the same time the mestizos are celebrating virginity ... what happens if the two functions collide in the street? ¡Ay-ay-ay!*)

September 23-24 Our Lady of Mercy Festival (Latacunga) Parades and parties follow religious processions.

November 2 All Souls Day (aka "Day of the Dead") Families visit cemeteries, to **dance, drink, eat** and leave flowers and other offerings.

November The Andean Highlands most important festival is the Mama Negra celebration (men dress up as black women), a pagan celebration dating back to the Spanish conquest.

December 6 Fiestas de Quito The first week of December Quiteños take in bullfights, parades, and street dances and ride around Quito atop *Chivas* (open-air party buses complete with live music and drinks).[9]

You get the idea.

Between the emotive Spanish legacy and the *indígenas* rich cultural heritage, there are endless reasons to process, petition, dance and parade in elaborate, richly-costumed ceremony. All the saints and ancestors and gods and Jesus and nature spirits and heroes and virgins and political liberators and miracles are to be feted in some illustrious manner. Making for an extraordinary eclectic mix, the indigenes embraced the heavy-in-ritual, European-imposed Catholicism and simply tacked on their pantheistic beliefs (double the divinity), the syncretism so nicely dovetailing as to be archetypal uncanny: Virgin Goddess/Virgin Mary;[*] Ancestor worship/All Saints Day; Sun Solstice/God Birth.[†]

"The innate, ancient reverence of the native soul finds a Christian outlet ... but the intention has remained the same over the millennia: to ask Mother Earth for her fruits, the Sun for his light, the Sky for rain, and ancient and new divine powers for their protection."[10] (Mario Polla)

Whether some performances we are fortunate to stumble upon are staged for tourists or authentic cultural display is hard to discern—I imagine it's both. Regardless, throughout the year Latin America and their indigenous cultures often engage in grand exhibition, often life-enriching, emotive display.[‡]

---

[*]   I've never understood what the big deal is with *virgins*—adoration across the board by nearly all cultures!—why? And the men try so hard to make it not so...! (by de-flowering)

[†]   Christian invaders are known to superimpose their religious observances over the existing indigene calendar of worship, harnessing the energy of the previously established pagan ritual. Hence the winter solstice/Jesus birth coinciding.

[‡]   I truly experience a reverse cultural shock when I return home from these travels and step outside into my conservatively-hued neighborhood (predominately beige) to find almost nothing going on ... save someone mowing the lawn.

151

The Downside View of a Passing-Through Traveler

From the superficial perspective of an outsider I am most blissfully unaware of the day-to-day struggle of grinding poverty—whether it is the city dweller or the *indígenas* living in the high Sierra. Through her volunteer work, Carly gained a keener insight, seeing firsthand the sores of child field laborers and their eagerness, their *need* for food. Ecuador is one of the poorest of all the Latin American countries (Bolivia holds the title) and throughout our journey there is much evidence to support that claim.

Within the last century there has been a major migration of rural populations—globally and most accelerated in Latin America—the peasant *campesino* worker flooding the larger cities in search of sustainable living; the megatropolis is a historical first.

> During the last fifty years the process of urbanization in Latin America has been remarkable. Whereas in 1950 less than 41% of its population lived in urban areas presently, that proportion reached about three quarters (United Nations, 2000) ... Urbanization in Latin America increased in fifty years (1925-1975) from 25.0 to 61.2% currently the proportion of people living in urban areas reached 75.3%.[11]

One result of this massive migration is an explosion of unimaginable, endless shanty towns (Lima, Sao Paulo, Mexico City, Buenos Aires) and clearly evident urban (as well as rural) poverty. There is an untold amount of laborers forced by economic pressure to emigrate both internally and transnationally (within the continent as well as to Western countries). I have read that the cost for hiring an illegal transport from Ecuador to the U.S. runs from $10,000 to $12,000 per person. This is unimaginable considering their extreme impoverishment. Ironically, Ecuador is reported to be a country rich in natural resources, but corruption, mismanagement, multinational exploitive practices such as in oil, mining, corporate farming etc. are said to exact a heavy toll. Apparently, because of these overpowering forces, small farmers can no longer eke out a living to support a family.

When I see for myself and bemoan the painfully obvious fact of the environmentally destructive urban congestion, of heavy brown skies filled with exhaust fumes, and just when I'm thinking *I'm grateful my home is so much cleaner and nicer* the realization hits me: the United States is second only to China as the worlds worst carbon dioxide polluter. Current 2014 World carbon emissions in billions of metric tons: China, 8.7; United States, 5.5; and Latin America, 1.3.[12]

I have to be mindful of an illuminating perspective I gained from attending a November 2011 lecture by Dr. Jane Goodall: Developing-world carbon footprint is nothing compared to that of a person born in the U.S. "We in the developed world have lived too long far beyond our environmental means," stated Dr. Goodall.

> With just 5 percent of the planet's global population, Americans consume some 30 percent of the world's material resources and 40 percent of gasoline. If everyone consumed like the average American, some scientists predict that we would need at least four more planets to provide the neccessary resources and absorb the waste.[13]

And yes, I am aware I took a plane to get South America, a major carbon excess.

One invariably catches sight of heart wrenching, serious maladies: unattended, shocking deformities of beggars; painfully meager, shanty housing; extraordinarily impoverished children; the destitute curled up in any crevice for a night's sleep; acrid fumes wafting from a sea of antiquated cars; a perplexing affinity for mindless trashing (particularly the garbage strewn along and within waterways)*; and, as most everywhere, the curse of alcoholism. Of course, all of these problems can easily be found here in the states, perhaps the occurrence not as blatant. (For example, chemical pollution of our water is a lot more discrete.)

---

* The result, I am told, of poverty in survival mode and lack of education. Imagine what your city would look like if there were no money for efficient garbage removal or enforced sanitation laws.

And there is all the **unpredictability**: Unreliable services, schedules, vehicles, energy (black-outs) and infrastructure, lack of safety standards (seatbelts, airbags) etc., etc.

The reputed ill-treatment of animals. Though I have not experienced it first hand, the prevalence of spike-enhanced cockfighting as *sport* is undeniably popular. This kind of bloody exhibitionism is certainly not for me (ditto for the bullfighting). We in the U.S. have illegal, underground problems with animal-cruel sport practices (Michael Vick, football sports icon, prosecuted in 2007 for an illegal dog fighting ring) as well as the perpetuation of unlawful cockfighting. In fact, I was shocked to learn that as recently as 2007 cockfighting was still legal in two U.S. states.

From the numerous accounts I've read detailing Shamanistic practices that include animal abuse—i.e., pummeled and skinned *cuy*; sacrificial pigs, llamas, llama fetus, etc.—leave me cold. I find the insensitive slaying of creatures for magical purposes abhorrent—and certainly distracts from any illusion of charm.

We were specifically warned to stay away from Otavalo's weekly livestock exchange, the severely shackled spectacles of livestock markets said not to be for the tender-hearted. (And easy for me to decry when I buy my flesh/protein from shrink-wrapped packages in a supermarket, oblivious to and cushioned from the invariable bloodshed involved.)* Our mostly corporate-run business of mass-produced, cramped warehousing of our live domestic food supply is without a doubt ethically questionable, if not wholly untenable.

Crime. Though—knock on wood—we have not been victimized having now traveled through six Latin American countries, the well-publicized, high crime statistics and the warnings issued by The U.S. Department of State International Travel site for most of Central and South America certainly gives one pause for concern.

---

* As I was writing this, the jarring revelation did occur to me that I am not one generation from severing chicken heads and hand plucking them myself.

On the streets it is dispiriting to see our Western-style pop culture and corporations infiltrate everything (the lure of pop culture seems irresistible worldwide'). The ubiquitous Coca Cola® signs and all our fast food enterprises pop up everywhere. In the larger cities you find Kentucky Fried Chicken, McDonalds, Burger King, Starbucks, Pizza Hut, etc., and American logos like Nike and Adidas are omnipresent (I once saw an *indígena* woman, minding her stall, with a rapper "Eminem" baseball cap on). It is disturbing and unfortunate to see this aspect of globalization (homogenization). We tourists are a double-edged sword, often essential for the economic benefits but contaminating the very thing we've come to see.

On a day-to-day basis, there's much to be grateful for here in the U.S.: our vast opportunities and freedoms; things like sanitation, efficiency, reliability in law enforcement, healthcare, safety standards, etc.—not to mention political stability (Ecuador had seven presidents in a ten-year span between 1996 to 2006). Specific to our small experience in Ecuador, the taken-for-granted services like dependable power and infrastructure, the extraordinary luxury of a hot (or even slightly warm) shower! (I imagine if we stayed in the four-star accommodations this isn't an issue.) Carly never got used to the bone-chilling experience of a cold shower in a cold climate. (Though it was energy efficient because you quickly got the hell out!) And certainly we missed all the non-smoking regulations: Developing-world cigarette smoking is, unfortunately, on the up swing compared to the declining statistics here in the U.S.

However, so many aspects of Latin American cultures are well worth experiencing and deeply enriching in so many ways! (Or else why would we, or anyone else, go?)

Though Hemingway was reflecting on Paris (and he lived a good part of his life on his Cuban hacienda *Finca Vigía*) a remark he made perfectly struck home with me as to how I feel when I experience certain other cultures (including some in Europe): "Paris is so beautiful that it satisfies something in you that is always hungry in America."[14]

---

*   For example: In 2012 Carly was on a tiny island off the coast of Vietnam, taken by locals to visit their hut-dwelling family. In the sleeping area of a young girl she finds a small shrine made in honor of … Taylor Swift.

I guess that's how I feel. There is a hard to define quality, a mysterious *something* missing here (at least for me). I often get the impression other cultures have a better handle on how to celebrate *daily* life; at being in the present rather than perpetually future-focused.' Some years ago I had a distinct revelation: there is no home plate; we endlessly run the bases. Consumerism demands that we *never feel satisfied*. The European-style café societies (including many of that style in Latin America), Spain's Tapa Bars, Europe and Latin America's glorious central plazas and open markets exhibit a colorful joie de vivre, of multi-generational community; the *art of living* through shared food, music and family. Not to idealize too much—there's a downside to everything—but still …

I suspect our intense consumerism and comfortable isolation has come at some cost to our souls.† I *would think* this is simply reflective of *my life*, but I continually run across the very same sentiment in countless travel accounts by Western authors. We have missed the joy of a row boat by erroneously thinking a yacht is the ultimate goal. I'm not suggesting scraping by with bare essentials is preferable (though there are happy people who do this too) but perhaps we can learn something from each other, mining the wisdom from both worlds.

---

*   I once had a *Porteña* (Buenos Aries resident) tell me she could not begin to grasp the American concept of "coffee to go." "Ludicrous!" She explained, "Drinking coffee is meant to be savored, as a social pleasure!"

†   I am reminded of this paucity of spirit when patronizing a super-sized box store such as Costco. In the face of such over-the-top abundance I look around to invariably see mostly dulled, cheerless faces. It seems almost no one wants to be here. Ironic.

A FAMILIAR THEME

After struggling with my clarity of thought, I came upon Jeff Rasley's *Bringing Progress to Paradise*, about his time spent in a mountain village in Nepal, and who I believe put things much more succinctly. On page thirteen he elucidates his belief about how life propelled by consumerism has resulted in "anomie and alienation"; we have the ability to improve the material life of the indigenous poor, but we lack their sense of relationship to each other and to the Earth.

> ... People living in traditional communities are defined more by relationships and what they produce and create, rather than by what they consume. This strikes a deep chord in those of us who feel the loss of the emotional honest and interpersonal warmth of an organic community.

> There is an attraction between Western and traditional cultures and peoples. Indigenous people desire what we have and we desire what makes them who they are. We have what will improve their lives in a material sense. But they have something we want: their sense of place, groundedness, and wholeness. Unfortunately, this relationship, even with the best of intentions, has too often resulted in destruction and distortion of indigenous culture.[15]

In Carl Hoffman's 2004 book *Lunatic Express* he travels for five months on the most dangerous means of public transport that exist in the entire world, from Indonesian ferries to cliff hugging buses in Ecuador. Upon returning home to the States—the last leg of his journey involves a Greyhound bus ride from L.A. to Washington D.C.—he expects to find familiar, comfortable solace, the joy of smooth, clean efficiency, but instead he is shocked to find it is *here* he experiences the most dismal, cultural poverty of all.

> We hit Vegas that afternoon, and America seemed like the saddest place I had seen in months. The worst, most

dangerous conveyances in the world always had a mix of people on them, people bursting with life and color and friendliness ... all those people had been so filled with generosity and spirit, curiosity about a stranger, and they all in some way had felt connected in a way they didn't even realize to a larger society, culture, family. But the people around me seemed alone, disconnected ... We were a bus of lost souls in a country that seemed without a soul ...[16]

Consider the contrast between the openness of the people, the nutritional homegrown, freely-shared peasant food he had enjoyed on developing-world transports to the wasteland of (high sodium, sugar, and fat) fast-food the Greyhound bus patrons consumed. Noting an unkempt male in black t-shirt playing a heavy-metal "Death" refrain, he goes on to experience the shock of everyone's alienation, the course antagonism, the isolated texting (his female seatmate immersed in *sexting*)—almost a denial to anything joyful or life affirming. What happened?

From author Linda Leaming in her 2011 book Married to Bhutan, she submits that Americans have veered off-course as to what brings happiness:

The Bhutanese are not very good at making money, but they are happier than Americans ... But once you take the road to happiness—the road less traveled, or the open road, or whatever you envision as our route to bliss—you have to be ready to face some discomfort. Ironically, this will make you happier.

We are hopelessly addicted to comfort in the U.S. I submit that comfort is a diversion, and it is not related to happiness ... we can no longer intuit that small is beautiful and less is more. Our recent economic problems drove home the point. The way we live is unsustainable. Now we're all beginning to see.[17]

Perhaps there is a shift of consciousness happening in the world? That we are finding the promised utopia of excess materialism to be hollow; that there is a better and different path for all. From a 2010 interview by Mark Szotek, the expertise of Dr. Jane Goodall:

> With rapid economic development, and large populations of people in nations like China seeking "their share" of the natural resources in the rest of the developing world—just as Europe had, just as America is doing—and with all the powerful nations wanting to exercise their right to their share of Africa's, Asia's, South America's resources, wild areas and forest face unparalleled threats, and the local people find themselves relegated to poverty as competition for global resources heats up to reckless levels. Ultimately, there are no real winners in this competition, as we all lose out if unsustainable economic practices lead to global environmental chaos. The hollow pursuit of materialism for its own sake is crushing to the human spirit. What will future generations think of a people who had trouble thinking beyond the next shareholders meeting?[18]

I will never forget the image of astronomer Carl Sagan in the 1980s *Cosmos* book and series, standing before an oak tree and proclaiming that we humans are made of the same "stuff" as the tree. Plants, animals, human beings share identical components that make up *all life* on earth. Our very bodies reflect the same patterns and structures repeated throughout the universe.

"… there are obviously wide implications, biological-evolutionary as well as philosophical, in the discovery that precisely in the chemistry of our consciousness we are kin to the plant kingdom." [12] (Peter T. Furst)

Ayahuasca (aya wah ska)

I am endlessly fascinated by the use of psychoactive plants found in Amerindian cultures, ancient or otherwise. However much I would like to present an authoritative history of the ethnobotanical research concerning the use of consciousness-altering plant substances I can't. I'm not remotely qualified. But I can repeat what I find interesting! I did learn there are oceans of words written on the subject by such intrepid scholars as the late Harvard Professor Richard Evans Schultes—of whom I have just become aware—and learned new concepts and words like entheogens (psychoactive substances or plant pathways to god or other spiritual dimensions) and ethnobotany (the study of culture and botany, investigating the complex relationships between people and plants).

So … a few notes on what caught my interest. First, from the astounding Amazonian explorer Dr. Richard E. Schultes:

> It is interesting to note that the New World is much richer in species employed as hallucinogens than the Old World. There are probably 150 species (including fungi) so used in primitive societies in the Americas …

> In any consideration of hallucinogenic plants it is essential to remember that primitive societies believe these psychoactive plants to be the "medicines' par

---

excellence, and that their unusual activity which puts man in contact with the spirit world … is due to a resident spirit or divinity. They are considered sacred medicines, not to be abused or taken merely for pleasure.[20] (Schultes)

New World belief systems (magico-religious) from the Mayans, Aztecs to Incans have a well-known history employing a variety of psychoactive substances. Many Amerindian cultures have utilized their native plants consciousness-changing powers for millennia. For that matter, the use of consciousness-altering plants has a worldwide ancient history now thought to *potentially* include Neanderthals by the discovery of particular flower pollens found in ceremonial graves. (What is alcohol, after all, if not a plant-derived consciousness changer?) It seems obvious we humans are inexorably driven toward a desire to alter our consciousnesses (excuse me while I get some more coffee, or as the Lakota visionary Black Elk called it, white man's *Black Medicine*).

Every time I have encountered an indigene culture to the south, there is a mind-altering plant substance historically and/or presently in use. Just to name a few selections: Incas with coca and vilca (who introduced Ecuador's Cañaris to coca chewing); Mayan and Aztec with mushrooms and peyote; Ananazi/Hopi with mushrooms and morning glory seed; Comechin and Condorhuasi of NW Argentina with cebil or vilca. Even uncured tobacco in large doses can be a hallucinogen, the smoke believed to carry spiritual power. The list is extensive. (In the case of the coca leaf chewing, its effect a mild buzz, a pleasant numbing and hunger suppressant said to help the poor Andean cope with a very harsh, physical existence.)

> When anthropologists, botanists, missionaries and explorers began pushing their way into Central and South America in the nineteenth and twentieth centuries, what struck them most about the spiritual practices they encountered was that they were almost always accompanied by the use of powerful plant hallucinogens.[22] (Andy Letcher)

The Abrahamic religions (Judaism, Christianity, Islam), known to ban their use and place intermediaries (as in clergy) and authoritative scripture between direct spiritual guidance or knowledge. (Hence the ensuing missionary battle on the ground, still in progress.)

It is important to note these are not the super-synthesized, out of context, version that make their way to our streets for the sole purpose of getting high—the indigene process often monitored by a maestro, shaman or *curandero* (healer) using time-honed ritual for guidance. (Not to say there weren't/aren't unsavory aspects/abuses as well.) Throughout time the dissemination is often controlled by a select group.

Now that I have inadvertently stumbled upon the entheogen ayahuasca—its origins lay within the Amazonian jungles—*I seem to encounter it everywhere!* Kind of like when you buy a new car, say a Prius, and suddenly the world is full of Priuses!

A quick Internet search reveals the mysteries of the Amazonian tribes' centuries-old ayahuasca decoction were sampled years ago by world renowned musicians, and the use common knowledge today among radio talk show hosts like George Nory (Coast to Coast); featured on television—I watched Discovery channel contributor Les Stroud take a 2010 on-camera dose-trip in the Peruvian jungle; and an online article/ video produced by National Geographic by writer/partaker Kira Salak. Apparently it is the *drug du jour,* a popular draw for Western tourism these days in South America, to call on the plant spirits for their psychic healing powers.

The liquid decoction of ayahuasca is derived from several Amazonian plant species. The word ayahuasca means *Vine of the Dead* (apparently "dead" is not such a bad thing) or *Drink of the Soul* and the recipe is so complex experts consider it a wonder primitive peoples ever mastered it. (Curiously, the native users report the living jungle plants communicate with them, *teaching* them the ways of its use.) Ayahuasca is said to be used as a learning tool, for direct connection to the spirit world—though [WARNING] traumatic, terrifying encounters can also be part of the package! That is why I will never take it.

As the uninitiated, I struggle mightily through the inadequacy of words, really the *human language barrier*, to understand the transcendent experience produced by ayahuasca (or transcendence produced by any other means): I simply cannot imagine what it must be like to feel unequivocally at one with the universe, to feel your molecular structure to be the same as *all*, and to seemingly have worlds appear beyond our five senses. Quoting from Gordon Sumner's (aka Sting) 1987 book, *Broken Music*, after consuming ayshuasca:

> I seem to be perceiving the world on a molecular level, where the normal barriers that separate 'me' from everything else have been removed, as if every blade of grass, every nodding flower is reaching out, every insect calling to me, every star in the clear sky sending a direct beam of light to the top of my head. This sensation of connectedness is overwhelming. It's like floating in a buoyant limitless ocean of feeling that I can't really begin to describe unless I evoke the word love ... Everything around me seems in a state of grace and eternal.[23]

The experience is said to open up the top of the head to allow universal energy/information to flood in, to clearly illuminate other dimensions, spirit worlds, and alien beings, as well as at times enabling you to fly. (As bizarre as science is now finding our Universe or Multiverse to be—with the possibility of infinite worlds and countless dimensions—who knows what *reality* is? Our inner cosmos is proving just as complex and fascinating as the outer ... and in the end, all of the same origin). Again, I must stress, there are also numerous ayahuasca reports of encounters with hideous screaming creatures, black tunnels to hell and the devil, and lots and lots of snakes—inner and outer. (Part of the self-learning process.)

Author Tahir Shah under the influence of ayahuasca, felt he understood the mystery of Peru's famed Nazca lines by physically/spiritually flying over them; all became clear as to why the enormous, ancient geoglyphs were created. (The complete designs—such as expansive illustrations of a hummingbird or a long-tailed monkey—were discovered by a pilot in the 1940s, their entirety perceptible only by air.)

Perhaps there is much untapped potential in stepping out of the limitations—the prison if you will—of our five senses. Frances Crick, co-discoverer of the DNA double helix, was widely rumored to have experimented with LSD, a DMT (dimenthyltryptamine) cousin of ayahuasca. Could controlled hallucinogenic use facilitate some valuable insights? Even Deepak Chopra admitted to sampling LSD at one time.

Oddly, or appropriately, as I am reading the neuroscientist Dr. Jill Bolte Taylor's book *My Stroke of Insight* detailing a massive stroke she suffered in 1996 that debilitated her left brain hemisphere, destroying her language skills and reducing her to predominantly right brain function, she also describes experiencing a feeling of euphoric cellular oneness with the universe that is remarkably similar to Sting's rendition. From Dr. Taylor: "My consciousness soared into an all-knowingness, a being at one with the universe ..." "[I] ... was completely entranced by the feelings of tranquility, safety, blessedness, euphoria, and omniscience."[25]

It seems I must find a way, naturally (without ingesting something or suffering a severe head trauma) to temporarily stop the incessant chattering of the left brain, to open to, and to dwell in, the peaceful transcendent light of the right brain.

In January of 2012 I received a dinner invitation for an opportunity to spend an evening's conversation with an ayahuasca enthusiast. Ten of us sat spellbound over a candlelit dinner as we listened to this doctorate-educated man tell of his thirty-one ayahuasca experiences ... and counting. Interestingly, when initially asked if he would be willing to share his experiences with us (for the most part a group of strangers that included, for him, a 150-mile drive over a snowy mountain pass at night) he replied that not only was he willing, but he considered it a *responsibility* to do so.

Before beginning, he prefaces his personal account of ayahuasca use, once again, with the inadequacy of words to describe it. Just as mystics or drug experimenters (*psychonauts*) have expressed throughout time, there's a fundamental inadequacy of the human language to convey the ineffable nature of spiritual (or hallucinogenic) transcendence.

I listen carefully and jot down notes as he begins his ayahuasca story: Some time after swallowing the liquid, he describes the onset of powerful, rolling, "waves of epiphanies ... healing waves ... liberating epiphanies" each becoming stronger than the next until reaching a point of *pure beingness* of "nothingness." He is acutely "aware I'm here" and then—**PREGNANT PAUSE**—perceiving "SOMEONE ... ELSE ... IS ... HERE." He becomes conscious of an*other* entity; an entity that has *always* been there, that is "a source of wisdom separate from me but inside of me." And from that entity (for lack of a better word, he remarks) "a sense of being taught by a *totally different soul*, teaching me without malice, filled with love." When this powerful influx of learning becomes too overwhelming for him, he senses another, less omniscient being, a helper "for lack of a better word you might say *angel*" to help him assimilate the immense outpouring of teachings.

He then pauses to stress "The Four Truths of Ayahuasca: Mother, Teacher, Vine of Death, and Vine of Soul." The source of this learning, he says, not the "rough, knock you around" experience of other drugs but that of the "Gentle Mother of all visionary teaching plants."

Taking questions from our group, he is asked about his ayahuasca-gained perception of good and evil: "There is no bad," he asserts, "this concept thrusts you into duality."

Someone else questions, Do plants have consciousness? "That has already been proven in the seventies," he believes. (The spirit of the jungle's Vine of the Soul is claimed by *ayahuasqueros*—purveyors of ayahuasca—to telepathically communicate with them.)

In support of his revelations, he suggests the act of "creativity" as a commonplace example—such as when an artist feels as though working with an*other entity*, as an energy coming *through* them.

Furthermore, he believes without a doubt, we are in a consciousness-changing transformation period here on earth.

I ask if he has any fear of death: "I don't want to experience [the pain of the] dying process ... but *no*." I follow with, "Is there consciousness afterwards?" He genially shrugs, as though this is utterly insignificant.

So, in conclusion, what to take away from his experience, how could we apply his perceived wisdoms to daily life? "Just celebrate … the energy that is freely given all around you," he responds with a beatific half-smile.

After his presentation, a discussion ensues around the table. There are those voicing support of an extant universal field of intelligence, giving as example the brilliant ideas achieved (and/or accessed) by the exceptional intellects that have walked among us—from the physicists trying to determine a universal principle to (seemingly) preternaturally gifted composers, luminaries such as Einstein, Newton, Beethoven, and Mozart. However, a valid point is stressed: the groundwork had been laid by most "geniuses" through disciplined toil and mastery of subject (the prepared mind). Nevertheless, some fantastic accomplishments said to be *revealed* to them as if from another source. (Intellect and intuition?)

> Einstein once said that while Beethoven created music, Mozart's "was so pure that it seemed to have been ever-present in the universe, waiting to be discovered by the master." Einstein believed much the same of physics, that beyond observations and theory lay the music of the spheres—which, he wrote, revealed a "pre-established harmony" exhibiting stunning symmetries. The laws of nature, such as those of relative theory, were waiting to be plucked out of the cosmos by someone with a sympathetic ear. Thus it was less laborious calculation, but "pure thought" to which Einstein attributed his theories.[25] (Arthur I. Miller)

On the other hand, the genius factor declared completely (corporeally) explainable. From *Genius Explained* by Michael J.A. Howe:

> One way to make progress towards explaining the human attainments that result in their creator being seen as a genius is to discover how a person masters the knowledge and mental skills that make those accomplishments possible. … In principle at least, there are no points at which explaining human accomplishments

> becomes impossible except by resorting to miracles or magic. .... It is entirely conceivable that geniuses are indeed born with special characteristics that partly account for their outstanding achievements.* [26]

As I understand it (always questionable), there are complex and countless dimensions and variables of genius that may never be understood (consider the extraordinary skills of the savant). Whether intellect, intuition or unusual access to existing information plays a predominant role, the emphasis remains with the intense efforts and prepared mind of the revered genius. It seems persistence, fierce determination and single-minded focus (i.e., hard work) cannot be avoided. *(Dang.)*

At the close of our discussion, an MD in attendance focuses in on me and my probing inquiries. She suggests that I should pursue the *experience* of transcendence (or at least some degree of an altered state) as words are innately a limiting, definitive dead-end. Not that she was advocating ayahuasca or any other drug use, but rather recommending the multiple ways to achieve similar results *naturally*. She confirms for me that DMT (dimenthyltryptamine), the active ingredient in ayahuasca, (also the chemical effect said to be activated by our brains in near death experiences) occurs naturally in our bodies, and thereby potentially accessible. Disciplined meditation (*meditation! meditation! meditation!*) is at the top of the list though there are other avenues, both contemporary and ancient. Yoga, Qigong, fasting, auto-hypnotic effect of prolonged, repetitive rituals such as tribal/religious chanting, drumming and dancing, are a few examples of traditional tools used to achieve a visionary or altered state. It seems humankind has been trying to throw themselves into a trance from the very beginning. (*And why is that a natural proclivity?*)

However, that there are several natural alternatives is good news because I am far too neurotic to ever try ingesting anything. I know this; *it wouldn't be pretty.*

---

* I came across an interesting theory of Einstein's genius stating that he was extraordinarily capable of accessing and utilizing the properties of both his left and right brain hemispheres, thereby using logic and imagination to hitherto unknown potential.

So, at the end of the evening, and before I start talking to trees, I had to know, Do plants actually communicate with us? I turned to my basically conservative, apple-orchard-growing husband who had little to say all evening and ask in jest, "Does this help you with your tree growing business?" His reply caught everyone by surprise: "Well, I did have two trees I planted that I always felt a close connection to; whenever I went by them, I somehow *just knew* if they needed something." This connection, he clarifies, was beyond any physical indication of distress.

I couldn't believe it!—a thousand years of marriage and he failed to mention to me that he communicates with trees! Everyone at the table was beyond delighted by this unexpected revelation. He was the ultimate hit.*

---

*   I have always wanted to dance to beating drums around a bonfire all night long until I saw visions. I do after all, have 1/32,000 ounce of Native American blood coursing through my veins.

†   Because I am a shallow person this does not make me happy (half kidding). He always inadvertently does this to me because he's so affable and good-natured. It's like the time we went to visit our then college-age daughter (Carly) studying in France. I had practiced and practiced conjugating French verbs to try to communicate with her host family, hoping to make a good impression of American families. During dinner Mark somehow let it be known he liked to watch the inane TV sitcom "Married with Children" starring Al Bundy. The host Dad, Jean Pierre, was a big fan of Al Bundy and they stuck their hands in their pants, laughed incessantly about "el buuundeeee" and got along famously the rest of our stay. It was all over for me; I might as well have been invisible. So, after this tree-talking revelation, our guest of honor excitedly follows Mark out to his pick-up truck with some book recommendations for him— not me. Books I know he will never read … (fume)

Riobamba*

The four a.m. hotel transport (van) takes us back to the Manta airport. This feels so much safer—there are even seatbelts!—and proves uneventful compared to our harrowing experience of the taxi cab drive that got us there. For our next leg it is necessary to fly back to Quito (an elevation gain of over 9,000 feet from the coast) where we will then catch a bus to Riobamba. Once there we *intend* to take a world famous train ride through the Andes.

Heading off the coastal region and back towards Quito, the capitol and second largest city in Ecuador, our smallish plane must climb up, up, up and back toward the highlands known as the Sierras. Mainland Ecuador is divided into three regions: Coastal, Sierra and Oriente (Galápagos archipelago, 570 miles west off the mainland, another matter). Coastal is self-explanatory; Sierra denotes the high Andes Mountains that practically split the country in two from north to south—this area harboring populated valleys and plateaus like Quito; and "Oriente" meaning "east" portion, inclusive of the Amazon jungle region.

> **At the small Manta airport** I feel as though I have been acclimated by now, native-ized in my new light-weight tie-pants and my clearly native bracelet. Yeah, I'm local cool all right, when this *other mother-led* traveling family pulls up for their flight all sitting like INDIANA JOANS in the open bed of a dirty old pick-up truck. Oh man, this dark-haired mother and her three teenaged offspring (upper middle-class Italian I'm thinking) really trump one middle-straddling-lower class mother and two twenty-somethings arriving in a van. The very bravery to take on three teenagers alone puts her in rarified status!

Our under-an-hour flight lands us back in Quito and to my utter surprise the entire planeload of passengers bursts into applause upon our safe

---

* Riobamba, Tomebamba, Cajabamba and Vilcabamba ... my keen mind detects a pattern here! In Quechua "bamba" denotes a "pampa," that is a plain, field or *territorio*. So Rio bamba is a river territory; Tome bamba an ax or knife field; Caja bamba, probably from a Quechua word for "cold" or cold place; and Vilca bamba, a sacred place. (*Vilca* also the term for a *sacred* hallucinogen).

landing! Did something heroic transpire? A near miss with death and destruction of which I was blithely unaware? A safe landing such a rare occurrence? Exuberant applause upon touch down, I soon learn, is simply customary on many South American airlines. (We are to encounter the same custom in Spain on a different trip.) Quickly disembarking we then have a mad dash by taxi to the city's main bus terminal in order to make our ten a.m. connection. This modern, multi-storied, glassed facility is large and airy and resembles an international airport terminal more than a bus station. Through massive congestion and confusion, we race up the escalator where there are an infinite number of ticketing windows fronted by perplexing names like Atlántida, Express Atenas, Alausi, Panamericana Internacional, and hordes of clamoring people—we miss our 10:00 a.m. reservation by ten minutes. We are feeling stressed and some inter-personal-relationship conflict (squabbling) takes place. However, the interminable bus lines provide quick access to the next departure within a couple hours time—though we've lost our money on the missed transport.

We take two escalators down and down to the somewhat dank and dingy basement cafeteria, and into a kind of Latino food court. There are plenty of travelers and families, though we are the only Caucasians. We pile our backpacks on the one vacant table and try to determine which food stall is least likely to have an ill-effect on our gringa stomachs (unbelievably, none of us ever gets *too* sick from the food this entire trip). I am transfixed by the sweet bakery goods—which seem the most innocuous. Ah, the divine aroma of freshly baked sweet breads! I devour a delicious *pan dulce* (bread sweet) while the girls get cheese sandwiches and batidos.

Our entire incentive to reach Riobamba is to take the much touted open-air train ride through the High Andes heading toward Cuenca, our next destination. Riding on top of the rail cars is an Ecuadorian custom that began as a way to escape the heat of the enclosed carriage, but is now a major attraction. Brochures show beaming-faced travelers sitting on the roof of the rail cars (some brave souls precariously hanging over the edges), soaking in the majestic vistas of a once in a lifetime experience. (It is listed in the *1000 Things To Do Before You Die* book.) The catch in our plans is the requirement that you have to show your passport *in person* to secure tickets. After our five-hour bus ride—the bus was very clean, comfy and nice by the way—*we race* to the train station only to have the very last ticket purchased right in front of our eyes! They're sold out! It is explained that some of the cars are being refurbished and are temporarily out of commission, so there are even fewer seats than normal. We are all bummed but Carly is the most disappointed; it is the one thing she most wanted to do on this trip.*

Crestfallen, we make our way to our guide book's recommended hotel where we have reservations. It promises a rich and warm cultural experience with even a llama and a parrot on the premises. We hope at least memorable accommodations will help salve our disappointment. The taxi pulls up to a flat-roofed structure, desolate and dismal looking, made of rough and worn, charcoal-gray stone set within a highly questionable neighborhood. As usual, we must buzz for admittance. (Don't let that taxi driver leave!!!) The small "lobby" space is shadowed and dark with something like red velvet furnishings. I am not seeing any charm. And where are the llama and parrot? Nary a sign of them. No, things are not looking good. We sink further into despair.

All right, perhaps all is not lost … maybe the rooms will save us. We are led across a small inner courtyard to our rooms. Everything we see is a bit on the shabby side. A flimsy white door is unlocked and opens to two tiny rooms with a very low popcorn-spackled ceiling. We (especially me) are glum as we put our backpacks down and sit on the threadbare bed.

I suppose I can do this …†

But then (light bulb!) I wonder, *Are we really in fact stuck?* Gingerly, I approach a change in plans. Poor Carly has made all our arrangements keeping in mind a moderate budget and I am sensitive to and appreciative of her best efforts, so I very carefully broach the subject: "Maybe we should just keep going." We three in council weigh our options. We could take a night bus and at least be making progress towards Cuenca instead of wasting a night *just sleeping* here. From the little we have seen, Riobamba does not look that intriguing. (It is gray, overcast and threatening rain which doesn't help our

---

*   Carly, three years later, reviewing my writing: "I still feel sick about it."

†   In defense of our much-trusted guidebook, the accommodations were cheap, clean, and a good bargain for the young backpacker.

outlook either.) The whole idea was the unattainable train ride so maybe we should see if we can get out of our room reservations first?

Back to the small cavelobby. Mercifully, it is no problem whatsoever to cancel our rooms! Gleeful and relieved, we head back to our rooms to retrieve our backpacks. Now, it begins to pour down rain. We pause to talk to the only guests evident, a twentyish couple from Holland. They are happily playing a board game in the tiny common room, the beating rain now like timpani drumming like mad on the metal roof. Conversant in English, they explain that they too had hoped to take the train, but because they are on a several month journey they have the luxury of time to wait for opportune conditions. (The two are so complementary in looks—reddish hair, athletic and a bit pale complexion—we aren't sure if they are brother and sister or married. I want to ask but it seems a bit intrusive.) There is always a contingent, a subculture if you will, of young adult backpackers around. All kinds of European (British, German, French), Australian and American taking extensive South American ventures and traveling everywhere from Colombia through Peru to Brazil and offering each other advice on good deals, what to see and what to avoid. (My daughters put me in the in-the-know loop by youth association.) Considering the bad rep many of these countries have for danger, I'm surprised at the ease and popularity with which all these excursions are undertaken. These intrepid individuals scoff at the over-hyped perception of danger, commenting you just have to know where to go and not to go—but everyone usually has a story or two about "so and so" getting robbed by knifepoint, as do these two Dutch. *Shrug*, they gesture, just have to be careful, like everywhere …

TAXI! We dash out of there like bats out of hell and head back to the bus depot. Thankfully (?) we are able to procure bus tickets for that very evening: 7:30 p.m. to 1:30 a.m. But now, pray tell, what travails might this *autobús de la noche* (bus of the night) have in store for us?

With a couple hours to kill we head to the city center for food. Played out, with time-on-our-hands, deadpan faces after a battle of who wants what to eat and where, we settle on a middle-of-the-road cafeteria. (Courtney loses out on her bid for a burrito—not good for her Leo temperament.) All light oak wood and glass (smeared) we thought it had the potential to deliver good quality food. Not so much. I consume lukewarm milk and a soggy sandwich while, after eating a similarly mediocre selection, the girls dangerously face each other for a long period of time. Inevitably the sibling sparring begins.

Courtney: (Meticulously scanning Carly's face), "Have you been wearing your retainers?"

Carly: (Defensively), "WHY?"

Courtney: "No reason."

Carly: (Alarmed), "*Why do you ask* Courtney!? Do my teeth look crooked?"

The tension builds; I'm getting nervous.

Courtney: "Just the bottom ones. You have a Snaggletooth."

Carly: "SNAGGLETOOTH! *Cooo*urtney what are you saying!???"

Courtney: "Nothing … *Snaggle.*"

I'm cringing. *Oh noooo, now what's going to happen???* Get out the dueling pistols from the packs.

To my utter surprise, Carly, though somewhat rattled, starts laughing uncontrollably; it's a tears ~~and snot~~ producing response to Courtney's mean-but-funny wit.

"Courtney, you have to tell me if you are really *serious?* Do my teeth look bad?" she pleas.

I shoot Courtney a menacing "back-off" look.

"No, I was just kidding …………….. Snaggle."

"COURTNEY! You have to tell me!" Laugh, shriek, more snot. "MOM, do I have a Snaggletooth?" She envisions herself these past few weeks as unknowingly presenting a visage of white trash to all who have had the misfortune to gaze upon her.

And so it goes, for another half hour or so. Back and forth, forth and back. Laugh, snort, cry, and pleas for mercy.

Now, throughout the rest of our trip, whenever Carly gets inordinately bossy or uppity, Courtney fells her with one quick swoop: "Snaggle." Confidence eviscerated, Carly crumbles like a wet tissue. And it all starts again.

During the rest of our luncheon lull, I muse about an interesting character, smoking and sipping his *café con leche* (coffee with milk) all by himself on the covered sidewalk terrace. No one is around him save the passerby. He's a middle-aged man in a rumpled overcoat, shoulder-length, unwashed hair—all ruffled and thrown-back (looking like a chunky cross between Christopher Hitchens and Hemingway). *Yes,* he looks a brooding, serious writer-type. I imagine he is taking a break from his brooding serious work, slavishly written in a cheap, *típico* South American hotel room: dimly lit, wobbly ceiling fan, and dilapidated shutters opening to the chaotic Riobamba street scene below. Yes, I'm sure that's it. (I hope he didn't overhear us and steal my "Snaggletooth" story line.)

"THERE WERE THREE AMERICANS SITTING IN A DESOLATE RIOBAMBA CAFÉ. I COULD SEE THERE WAS A MURDEROUS RAGE SEETHING AMONGST THEM: THE TWO YOUNGER WOMEN CAPABLE OF THE MOST SINISTER VIOLENCE; THE OLD ONE CONSTANTLY TRYING TO PLACATE THE RAW EMOTIONS OF THEIR PERENNIAL SIBLING RIVALRY. I COULD HEAR THE INCENDIARY SLUR 'SNAGGLETOOTH' CAST ABOUT, IGNITING PASSIONS LIKE A BLOWTORCH TO A PARCHED DESERT."

Latino Pulitzer Prize winner 2012: *Diente Torcido* (Twisted Tooth) by Ernesto Hitchens. (Something's always lost in the translation.) Soon to be a major motion picture. (Flash to image: Carly's face on big screen, close-up centered on her one twisted tooth.)

LATER AT THE BUS DEPOT, around 6:30 p.m., I of course want to use the bathroom one last time before embarking on a purported six-hour bus trip. As I rush to the facilities, I am brought to a dead halt at the entryway by an imposing, stern-faced, tight-bun-on-her-head matron demanding something from me. *What?* I have no clue. Can't she see I am a helpless gringa? Nope, she will not back down or cut me any slack—or any toilet paper. I am barred from entering! Is she a warden in her day job? I have to run back to get some entry money and for her Extreme Highness of Royal Baños to dole out five whole squares of toilet paper to me! (Another example of how absolute power corrupts!) And believe me, the condition of the facilities are not worth even a pittance of pesos. (If only I could read Spanish to decipher the infinite amount of black marker messages scrawled on every square inch of the walls.)

I return and the bickering begins. The subject: who gets to sit with Mom? I wish I could say it is a fight born of untold fealty and adoration, but it is simply the fact that I serve as a big pillow and barrier to strangers. All crisscross routes painfully recounted it is determined it is Carly's turn to be my seatmate. Courtney fumes.

Departing the dank and dirty depot, we walk over the oil-besmirched, spat-upon' asphalt. However, we are pleased to find the bus interior in exemplary condition: it's clean, modern and much superior to our Greyhounds. What a nice surprise! There are even a few empty seats.

Midway into the bus, I grab a window seat, then Carly the seat next to me, then Courtney sprawls over two seats across the aisle from us. Knowing Courtney is in a foul mood, we are cautiously observing all on-comers, hoping beyond all hope they will bypass her extra seat. (The addition near the front of the bus of two young, languid and hip, backpacking British women, slightly assuages my anxiety about being the sole white foreigners.)† We hold our breath as each passenger boards, scans their options and passes Courtney by. When the doors close and no one has taken the seat next to her we breathe a sigh of relief; now we can all be happy! Halleluiah! (We had no idea the bus would stop a thousand more times on our night journey.)

---

* If I am ever ruler of the world I would make all public spitting a crime punishable by … by … having the perpetrator's person and properties spat upon by a large contingent of state-appointed, saliva-gifted dispensers of justice. *Oh no! Here comes the "Spit Busters Van"* (officially The International Expectorant Extinguishers Unit or *IEEU!*). *And they all have water bottles for reloading! RUN!*

† I came across a website warning as I was researching this portion: "Night buses not recommended because of hijackings and robberies." Who knew? Not us.

Courtney rolls and bundles herself up like a menacing little troll, with her hooded sweatshirt tied tight around face, wearing sweat pants and flip flops, and curled over two seats; no one dares to disturb her. (*I was afraid of her.*) She must've been emanating some pretty potent negative vibes. The closest encounter she has with a seatmate—and I apprehensively watch this all transpire—happens in the wee hours of the night. An aged indigenous man boards the bus from the middle of nowhere. He's large and weather-beaten, dressed in a heavy overcoat and soiled, floppy, felt hat. He lumbers down the aisle with clear intent on Courtney's seat. Tapping her on the shoulder Courtney's snarly face awakens (veritable hissing)— taken aback, the poor guy moves on down the aisle to safer territory.

Courtney: "I gave him my best evil stare."

> "We went like ten miles an hour on a dirt road under construction for another dirt road." –CG

Yes, what Courtney says is true. We creak and groan and back up and around road blocks at what seems a snail's pace. From my window seat I (bug-eyed) observe every square inch of the thirty-ton bus maneuverings as we back over and straddle a precipice daringly astride a deep construction pit. Both girls innocently drool and remain unconscious throughout. (One could never say "sleeping" because that would connote restful pleasure. No, this is more like a descent into a Dantean world of loony, nonsensical thoughts, involuntary startling, and barely below consciousness delirium. The *I think I slept but I'm not sure* kind.) We wait a half hour at this spot for the only other conceivable vehicle on the planet—another commercial bus—to traverse a one-way portion on this most desolate of country routes.

Fortunately, the bus company provides three, charming, delightful movies to distract us from any black danger lurking in the night.

SHOCK SPLAT X*!OxXXX PUKE NAUSEATING THUD X*!O~xX SLASH STEAMING BLOOD SPURT HOT GUTS BONE CRACKING GORE … AND THEIR HORSES TOO

They run three, back-to-back, horrifically violent Mel Gibson movies. Guck, hack, gurgle, slash, and last agonizing gasps—with only brief moments of respite. Unbelievable. I do my best to avoid letting any of this vileness seep into my visual cortex as I know Carly is too: when I turn to look at her I am surprised to find only a partial nose. She has creatively and elaborately wrapped and tucked her long, muslin scarf tightly around her head, face, and ears, looking not unlike a Bedouin mummy. (Courtney is still passed out). However, beyond my control are unintentional sightings, the occasional flash reflected in my window. UGH! *Nooooooo,* I accidentally view a bloody limb being hacked off!!!

WHO CHOOSES THESE MOVIES AND WHY????

I have since read other travel accounts stating this is pretty typical fare on long South American bus rides. Clint Eastwood, Sylvestor Stallone, Charles Bronson, and Bruce Willis films being other favorites. What?

Deep Dot Thought

It is beyond my capability to fathom why gory violence is considered entertainment. I experience nauseating revulsion. My mind ponders the big questions: why is it that simulating close-up gruesome, hellish massacres results in box office success? What dark corner of the primitive (reptilian) brain does gruesome slaughter stimulate, or even titillate? Do I possess this propensity buried deep within my DNA, needing only the right conditions to bring it out? Do women enjoy them as much as men or is this a dominant male thing? And why would anyone want to subject themselves to nonstop, gory violence on an all night bus through the dark hinterlands of Ecuador? As usual, I am profoundly mystified at human nature.

IT IS A FULL MOON and I am intrigued, drawn in by the passing moonlit landscape. Fortunately, we thought to bring along an iPod and I am listening to the *Book of Secrets,* the world music of Loreena McKennitt. Befitting and complementing the unknowable terrain, the music is transcendent; it's so spell binding and so *intensely* pleasurable I think because I have been without it for such a long time. I watch the desolate countryside roll by accompanied by her mystical, ethereal refrains. *Indígena* bus riders board and disembark from and to god-knows-where empty space. There's no apparent sign of life for miles on end. Adios, and where and what kind of life are you walking to down that dark road? *Qué misterioso.* (How mysterious.)

Every once in a while we come upon a small city or village, an oasis of light and life in what has become a nocturnal black sea. Of notable charm is the town of *Alausí.* After so much darkness it is quite unexpected to curve and curl, down and down into a valley, and in one blind turn, a radiantly glowing, enormous statue of Jesus appears. Placed on a bluff overlooking the city, it is all awash in light and seems to be hovering in the sky. The celestial illusion is one of startling beauty. As we pass through the city center, though it is late evening, we are surprised to find a vigorous soccer match being played by young boys upon a floodlit, green field. The city's cobblestone streets, their glowing cathedral, and white-washed stone buildings are all delightful images.

However, the scenes from our *bus route* window, when we do pass through populated areas, are predominantly images of ramshackle constructions, dismally-lit cafes, shoddy looking *tiendas* and tire stores, and an occasional sighting of locals gathered around outdoor fire pits for warmth.

I am not intending to disparage the country by painting negative visuals of poverty—our scenes of poverty are not any better in the U.S., but it is estimated that over half the population in Ecuador is considered impoverished and the cobbled-together use of industrial byproducts does not (for the most part) make for an aesthetic blend. I stumbled across this clarifying observation on a *Culture of Ecuador* website: "Regional architectural styles that rely on natural materials such as palm, mangrove, bamboo, and thatch on the Coast; with thatched roofs, eucalyptus, maguey stems, earth pampas grass and thatch in the Sierra; and palm, bamboo, and thatch in the Oriente, increasingly, these natural materials are being supplemented or replaced by cut planks, cinder-block, cement, brick, ceramic and asbestos tile, and corrugated metal." The overall effect and sprawl is not pretty. But clearly my myopic lens of perception is of a white, middle-class, foreigner.

I admire what looks to be a pleasurable and thriving social scene in the occasional town: men play cards sitting amongst their open-air tire shop;

families partake of an evening meal on crowded restaurant patios; and groups of *compadres* converse over beverages at gas station cafés. And always there's the free-wheeling male motorcyclist buzzing around it all, often with a female and/or extended family member clinging on to the back. I like all this and feel a twinge of envy at witnessing all the social camaraderie, thinking my gregarious husband Mark would so easily fit in and so readily enjoy this lifestyle.

There are plentiful evening hours for socializing. On the equator the sun goes down, like *bam*, every night around six p.m. There's no variation (well, a few minutes), no twilight, and no lingering sunsets. It's twelve hours of daylight and twelve hours of nighttime. That's it.

Though it is well past midnight, I catch sight of three indigenous men, sitting in a row, identically dressed in ponchos and knit hats, and all remaining *unnaturally still*—like inanimate specters hardly discernible beneath the beams of a crumbling veranda. For some reason, their frozen, lifeless demeanor—sitting partially hidden in the shadows as they are— strikes me as eerie. (Most likely, it is simply *my projection* from a major cultural barrier: a bus window.)

Nearing two a.m. we finally pull into Ecuador's third largest city, Cuenca, and immediately secure a taxi ride to the Central District. En route we are feeling intense trepidation as to what to expect for lodgings (our reservations having been made from the same guide book as in Riobamba). I am seriously, keenly studying the deserted streets and neighborhoods, worrying if the hotel is going to be decent and, above all else, safe—especially arriving at this very late hour. The narrow avenue we're traveling, filled with urban street scenes of modern and colonial structures, consists primarily of white-washed stone and cement buildings on stone and cement streets. Everything is secured, shuttered, locked and *bolted up tight*. From what I can deduce from a taxi cab window, our destination in the heart of downtown looks to be acceptable.

Deposited on an empty sidewalk, the taxi speeds away and there's not a soul in sight. First, we can't find the front door! This search takes time and there are a number of potential doors to bewilder us. Back and forth, forth and back we go. Yikes, I keep nervously checking over my shoulder into the shadows for any emergent characters of mal intent. Are we in the right place? *If not, then what do we do? Lurk in some crevice until daylight?* At last, Carly spots a barely discernible street number above the far door. This is it. We commence ringing the bell like crazies, but no one wants to answer. (Still plenty of time to be murdered.) At long last, a groggy and very grumpy clerk buzzes us in, and yes, it is the right place. Relieved, we throw our packs down and proceed to check-in. He continues to be ill-tempered. (*Sooooorreeeeyyy* we paying female guests worried about being completely vulnerable and assaulted on a dark street corner in the middle of the night disturbed you so!)

I critique the lobby while Carly does the registration translating. This looks very encouraging: attractive breakfast area of burgundy wood tables, grand staircase leading to an impressive upper floor balcony circuited by all twelve guest rooms, and an immense chandelier hanging below a fabric-draped, ceiling skylight. (The hotel used to be a colonial mansion in its day.)

With our keys distributed, we go upstairs to check out our accommodations.

Wow (bad *wow*) … this is nothing like the website photos. When planning the trip we had previewed some advertised images of spacious, elegant rooms with floor-to-ceiling flowing draperies around double-door shutters that open to private balconies. Instead, we are relegated to what must be their least desirable room. It's a completely cramped space of maybe ten by twelve feet with a double and single bed crammed into it—and no place whatsoever to put our things. But the insult upon injury is our window view: All beautifully curtained and shuttered all right … and opening directly onto … the interior walkway. Should we have the desire to become complete exhibitionists (not unlike a storefront window) we now have that appealing option.

Oh yes, a feeble goodnight wave to you Señor and Señora strangers, before turning off the bedroom light. Be sure to watch us awaken in the morning!

My face falls in disappointment. We are all travel weary and the girls curtly advise me to just accept and deal with it: "How long will we be here anyway? Just shut the curtains." But, I think a great room can be half the pleasure! As I try to get to the bathroom my ankles twist and turn amongst the strewn backpacks and cast-off shoes and I consider what a nightmare this is going to be for three whole days when we *really get disorganized*. Ignoring their advice, I quietly resolve to see what I can do about the room situation the next day.

I am a big believer in heartfelt sincerity, in honesty—what can it hurt? So, in the morning, I find a member of the hotel staff prepping one of their choice rooms, with an exterior view (!) of the San Francisco Plaza below. I graciously inquire if she would be so kind as to *at least let me see this room*. The late-fortyish mestizo women, who appears to be of a managerial status, invites me in as I *sincerely* lavish praise on this truly charming accommodation. (We are all paying the same price!) Seemingly pleased by my comments, she offers to show me their very best room of all: the double balcony, corner room. Gazing wantonly, forlornly at this gem, I describe our sorry circumstances … how I would probably never be in Cuenca again … how we were so looking forward to **the room that was pictured on the brochure**. I then lead her back to our room to witness our pitiful conditions.

Well. Though we had been tersely informed by the irritable hotel clerk, *all rooms were completely booked* for the entire weekend and there was *absolutely no chance of a change*, somehow a room miraculously opens up at the last minute! We get to move into the best of the best: The corner room with two double-door balconies. Halleluiah, we are ecstatic! (See girls, what did I teach you about sincerity/honesty?) Am I grateful for the empathy shown by that woman!'

Woo hoo! Now we have places for all our stuff, an armoire, chandelier, decorative wallpaper, a breakfast table, two exterior views and a spacious bathroom. NOW THIS IS A GREAT ROOM! I am happy!

---

* I came across a traveler's comments on a website concerning this hotel and having the same experience. What's the scam? I have since been informed that I, naïve, was probably supposed to grease the palms of those in charge in order to get a nice room. Not exactly Holiday Inn style; how was I to know?

Dorothy E. Groszhans

Quirks Típico of South America

We are so used to things working efficiently here in the U.S. it is an amazement when we encounter otherwise. Every day things like light switches. (Who thinks about them? I don't.) In our hotel, there is a long delay between turning the switch and receiving power—if it happens at all. First we think all our light bulbs are burnt out and request new ones. But no, the summoned employee deftly *maneuvers* the switch and successfully produces light! We feel like imbeciles. We then learn to *work the switches* in order to get a current going (not always successful), producing a *click-snap-zap-spark-click-snap-zap-spark*—an unnerving sound. In the quiet hours of the day or night we can hear all the other guests throughout the hotel doing the same thing: *click-snap-zap-bizzt-snap-zap-bizzt.* At least we know we aren't the only ones having trouble. Also—and this relates—the door to our windowless bathroom doesn't fit properly and has the tendency to firmly jam when shut. This anomaly results in the occasion of a panic-stricken, trapped-in-complete-darkness victim that can't get the timed lights (that turned off) to come back on again. "Help!" Pound, pound, pound. *Where did the girls go?* "Carly? Courtney?" Anybody, anybody? *How do I say "heelllllpp" in Spanish?* This is a very scary feeling!

(Unfortunately, this incident is true.)

When the girls returned from breakfast they had a lot of difficulty forcing the door open. Ugh. Thereafter we kept it ajar for ambient lighting.

Cuenca

Santa Ana de los cuatro ríos de Cuenca
or
Cuenca

Rise and Shine. After our typical hotel-provided breakfast of biscuits, jam, eggs and Nescafé (there's no one but us in the breakfast room, *where is everybody?*) we head out the always-locked hotel door, in search of real caffeine. We are located right on the San Francisco Plaza which appears as a market primarily for locals. On this non-market day, it's mostly an open parking lot of dark gray brick with adjacent gray and drab marketing stalls displaying familiar merchandise. Not the prettiest market we've seen by any means. However, after just a short stroll we are passing through a glorious flower market tended by local (mainly indigenous) women. Incredibly vibrant colors activate our senses, the richness of hue made more so by the contrast to the heavy overcast sky and stone gray setting. The air carries the heavy, humid scent of impending rain and the moisture adds a buoyancy and life to the spectacular, fragrant flowers. (The typical weather pattern in these high sierra regions near the equator is a year-round mild climate with the peak temperatures floating between the upper 50s and lower 60s, frequently producing sun and rain in the same day.)

Because of this favorable, gentle, sub-tropical climate, cut flowers are a major Ecuadorian export. (Check where your grocery store cut-flowers come from next time, it's a good chance from Ecuador or Colombia.) In this cobblestone plaza, *Plazoleta del Carmen,* set within the grace of an impressive church, my senses are swept into the vibrant current created by the lush color spectrum. There are a plethora of perfected blooms and extraordinary healthy flowers at their peak: multi-hued roses, chrysanthemums, calla lilies, sunflowers, stargazer lilies, hydrangeas, carnations, etc., etc., all but vibrating with color and life—and not a single wilted petal in sight. What an uplifting morning charge!

But first, we are on a mission for coffee. (Imagine what the flower market will be like *after* I've had caffeine!) Our guide book suggests a corner café within walking distance of our hotel

Part of the fun of traveling is finding a special spot, one that you can irrationally place your stamp on (scent?) and illogically call your own. *Café*

Austria becomes that for us. One of the highly valued places serving *real coffee* we feel a twinge of guilt whenever we look around to see most patrons are Westerners (of European descent) like us—not quite the local crowd. Still, the high ceiling and airy ambience of this wood-trimmed and stone building are wonderful. There's a long mahogany bar of fresh baked breads and desserts, an extensive list of espresso delights, cool jazz on the sound system, foreign newspapers, sumptuous food and a preponderance of warm wood tones throughout. All this set within spacious windows overlooking the city's bustling streets. Perfect. We plan our agendas over wonderful coffees, pastries, orange juice and batidos at a coveted window table. (It's a good thing we tend to walk like maniacs considering our high caloric intake.)

Carly has brought her guide book along so we can plot our three-day course. The suggestion of a day-long immersion into the local indigenous culture, the *Cañari*, jumps out to us as a perfect fit—especially when it is stated that the fee goes entirely to the benefit and maintenance of their culture. We will sign-up post haste for *Mamá Kinua's Kushi Waira!* The plan on the ground evolves into: First day, *getting to know Cuenca* by any means, whether by foot, bus or taxi; second day, full day *Cañari* immersion on site (forty minutes out of town); third day, taking in the citywide music and dance festival celebrating the *Bicentenario*—200-years of independence from Spain. More or less, *más o menos!* And whatever else comes our way!

Once sufficiently dosed with caffeine, we head out to face the days adventure. Skittering (lots of coffee) right past the seductive, rainbow-drenched shops of glorious textiles—hammocks, scarves, blanket weaves, hair wraps *(cintas)*—we set out to get our bearings. This is where Carly routinely performs what I call her "Prairie Dog Syndrome." First and foremost, we must find the highest navigable point in the area, march to the top where she can stand up on her hind legs, sniff the air, and determine her precise whereabouts in the ~~prairie~~ city. *After this essential orientation is complete*, we can go about our day. (Actually, it is good she does this since she invariably becomes our navigator. I tend to just wander around and around in a fog if left to my own devices.) Our hilltop viewpoint presents an open sea of terra cotta tile roofs under a tumultuous gray sky, punctuated by majestic cathedral domes.

Santa Ana de los cuatro ríos de Cuenca
(Saint Ana of the Four Rivers of Cuenca)

Wow, look at that full name of Cuenca! So what is it about that Spanish propensity for excessive flourish? This cultural trait is not neat and efficient! Names go on and on and on, sometimes even repeat the very same surname! like *Jesus Gonzalez-Gonzalez*. It is certainly un-American to be so name wasteful! It used to send me into fits when, as a teaching assistant, I was in charge of organizing, alphabetizing and filing all the adult ESL (predominantly Latino) student records. For example: *Conchita de Guadalupe Reyes Mirelez-Fuentes*. "Okay, so what is your last name?" I try to pin her down. *"No comprendo,"* responds the un-alphabetizable student. Not only that, several students would switch their string of names around at will, apparently as the mood strikes them. *La la la la, today I think I'll use Reyes, tomorrow I'll answer Fuentes, and after that Mirelez* ... just for fun—and to make that crazy lady even more crazy! I was so desperately trying to be Ms. Efficient it drove me bananas. YOU HAVE TO PICK ONE LAST NAME AND STICK WITH IT! I anguished for the integrity of the records! Met with a puzzled look by the offending student, it is finally explained to me that they honor the mother's heritage equally with the fathers ... so how can they choose?

Oh .... that's pretty impressive.

I hereby propose that my home town be renamed with much more flare:

Yakima

or

*Yakima of the one river and twin to Palm Springs**
Yakima of the one river abutted by two buttes
Holy Guacamole! only one river runs through it

Jakima del único río y gemelo de Palm Springs
Jakima del único rio a lado de dos buttes
¡Ay carumba! solo un río corre allá

Somehow it just doesn't sound as pretty.

---

* We have a notorious, floodlit billboard—erected by a private citizen—on a main thoroughfare claiming Yakima to be "The Palm Springs of Washington." Nothing could be further from the truth. Where are the palms? Where are the springs? Where are all the bejeweled glitterati? Mr. Meanswell, tear that billboard down!

We encircle the greater metropolis (a lot of walking and a lot of hills) partaking of a plethora of churches and monuments along the way (there are reported to be 52 churches in the historical district). Taking this in, it occurs me what a man's world we live in without being cognizant of it most of the time. All the monuments to men and their achievements (heavy on the warriors) makes me wonder how different, how strange it would be to encounter a city or a cathedral with a predominant homage to women. Just a thought. (It's the same experience in every country.) Is there a church anywhere honoring mostly females? Surely there has to be enough pious women to FILL ONE. Perhaps *the builders of monuments* honor their own?

During this trek Courtney and I are allowed mere nanoseconds to peruse the church interiors since, after numerous tours through Europe, Central and South America, Carly also suffers from CO Syndrome (Cathedral Overload) "been there, done that, can't take anymore" she says, and mocks how each one plays up some kind of obscure, one-of-a-kind feature. "The only church in the world to have *blah, blah, blah*" ... St. Francis' nose bone/eyelash/finger tip, a splinter from an apostle's soup spoon, the bit secured from Joan of Arc's horse. It is clear Carly is going to hell.

Santa Ana de los cuatro ríos de Cuenca is a charming city! At 8,200 feet elevation, it is one of the richest agricultural basins in the Ecuadorian Andes. As of a 2010 census, the urban population consists of about 330,000 souls and the greater metropolitan area, 500,000. The city center's historical zone was designated as a UNESCO World Heritage site in 1999; this translates into well-maintained, charming colonial buildings—some originating from the 17ᵗʰ century—magnificent churches, lanterns and flower baskets on cobblestone streets. (I noticed a minimal amount of the normally ubiquitous tangle of power lines, at least in this central district.)

It is considered one of Ecuador's most beautiful cities, competing with Quito for the title. Home to two universities, *The University of Cuenca* and the *University of Azuay*, the city has a thriving student population and is known to have produced some of Ecuador's most notable writers, poets, philosophers and artists. Along picturesque walkways, a grassy sloped *Tomebamba River* winds beneath opulent adobe housing—often with the spectacle of Indigene women washing and drying clothing along the banks. Add to that a rich selection of museums, galleries, thriving open-air markets, cafes and ... what more could you want? [22]

I would recommend this city to anyone.

By mid-afternoon we are ready to board the double-decker, open-air bus—to take in the high points. (Yes, it's touristy, but we've found interpretive tours to be informative, fun and a welcome break from incessant walking.) Guided through the town's main corridors of commerce, I am amazed at how European it all looks. From the breezy *autobús* upper deck, I gaze up with a crystal clear view of ornate and upscale second story apartments: flowers, wrought iron balconies, exquisite marble stonework, carved doors, quaint yet elaborate shutters, and expensive leaded glass—Old World design that *appear to me* to be a mix of French and Spanish styles. Below the apartments and lining the sidewalks, are high-end retail shops and a preponderance of urbane restaurants—all very contemporary and alluring.

Our day's home base revolves around the city's main square, that is, the palm trees, conifers, benches and fountains of *Parque Abdón Calderón*.

Here there is a glorious, bustling atmosphere of merchants and locals and tourists. Along the square, we find a suitable restaurant, *Raymipampa,* which meets our threesome's disparate needs. The interior has an oblong, dark wood, ground floor and upper balcony seating. Just outside the entrance, sidewalk merchants sell wares like bracelets and earrings and incense receptacles (clever ones of hollow bamboo with incense smoke pouring out the mouth of carved deity faces) that always snag my interest no matter how hungry I am. (Visual: Carly forcibly pulls me by the arm, away from the earrings and incense lures and into a late lunch.) Though the place is continuously slammed with hungry patrons, locals and tourists alike, the waiters are joyful, boisterous and welcoming.

Here we basically repeat our Puerto López pattern: Carly and I select healthy vegetarian food involving quinoa and potato-based soup; Courtney gets the best grilled chicken with a delectable special sauce, avocado, tomato and french-fries (though served with a strange Not-Heinz ketchup). I switch to Courtney's choice the next day.

Now, a major misnomer is the "Panama" hat. Why do I mention this? Because they are made in Ecuador; they have always been made in Ecuador. The plant used to weave the original Panama hat derives from the *paja toquillo* (Carludovica palmate), a palm-like plant that thrives in the central coastal region of Ecuador. Apparently, in times past, the uniquely woven, cooling hat became associated with a Panamanian distribution point and errant word of mouth. But it was, and continues to be, an Ecuadorian product (although now undermined by countless imitations).

We locate a downtown hat factory and store. Inside we find weavings in progress: long strands of unwoven, bleached and golden straw flailing out from half-completed rims. The walls of the long, cavernous shop are filled with various Panama styles and there are stacks of precious hats waiting *to be repaired.* If we were expecting some bargain basement deals, the high price tags, most deservedly on many of these time-consuming creations, quickly dash that notion. I learn that some of the finest handmade hats are the result of a months-long, fastidious process, and the work of superb weaving dexterity. Quality is measured by the fineness of the weave: the tighter the weave, the higher the quality. (To control the effect of humidity, some hats are said to be woven only in the evenings by moonlight!) Exquisitely suited to their environment, the cooling yet water-tight *Superfinos* are considered the very best, possessing the ability to be tightly rolled for storage (moisturizing first recommended) yet retain their form when unfurled (Beware: There are prolific, misleading *Superfino* labels!). Sigh ($$$—$$$$), learning of this intricate, masterly workmanship that produce the finest, authentic Panamas, I now appreciate *sombreros de paja toquillo* as wonders of human ingenuity. (The art of weaving the Ecuadorian *toquilla* hat was added to the UNESCO Intangible Cultural Heritage Lists in 2012.)

I will mention the one museum I peruse only for the fact that it is the first time I have ever encountered *tsantsas,* that is, shrunken heads.* At an impressive, multi-level museum, *Museo Pumapungo,* showcasing life-size dioramas of Ecuador's numerous indigenous cultures, shrunken heads from the Amazonian Shuars are a main attraction. (Heads-up!)

I'm all alone in a hushed museum room where incandescent spots highlight the heads in a glass-encased stand. Feeling a sense of unease and respect for a human life, I gaze, mesmerized by the mass of thick black hair and long eye lashes on one tiny gnarly face, and the painful spectacle of sutured together lips, long remnants of the thick white string cascading down like mouth froth. (Ow!) Apparently, the binding of lips is to prevent the malevolent spirit, the *musiak,* from escaping and exacting revenge. So strange to contemplate that this was once an actual person ... father ... brother ... son ...uncle ... now preserved in perpetuity ... viewed under artificial sunlight ... by an alien white woman ... in the year two thousand and nine ... flying here from five thousand miles away. Imagine if this person had been foretold of his (head's) physical destiny?

---

*   Did you know that shrunken heads are a highly sought after collector's item—a *lively* illegal and underground market exists? I know this from one book I read, *Trail of Feathers* by Tahir Shah and a television show I watched. Again, what's with human nature? I've seen pictures of collectors wearing a *tsanta* as a **necklace!** And how do you coordinate with the rest of your outfit? Eye-teeth earrings? A denture-clasp broach? A femur bone hair wrap? A quiver of diamond studded blow darts? I guess I could always hang one with a strand of garlic in the kitchen ... *oops* I meant to put garlic in that dish! *Oh well, the luncheon ladies will never know ...*

Gracing the entryway towards the room honoring the ancient art of pottery, written in elegant script are the words: *tierra, agua, aire, y fuego*. The elements of all pottery: earth, water, air and fire. I'd never thought of it that way before. The Spanish words catch me with their poetic beauty. I fall into dreamy thought, pondering human evolution and visualizing the intrinsic beauty of each element. *Tierra, agua, aire y fuego;* the elements of all pottery, the elements of all life …

* Our very selves having arisen from this universe/earthen mix

* Our species commandeering this life-force to astonishing new heights

* The marvel of consciousness, of human expression

* Fire the stored energy of a star, our energy-source

* How stunningly beautiful our whirling-blue home planet …

Okay, so snap out of it. There's still a lot more to see!

A mystery: According to Noam Chomsky, MIT Institute Professor and Professor of Linguistics (Emeritus), the impetus for our transition from inarticulate creatures to ones who become spectacularly creative—whether through manipulating the environment (earth, air, fire and water) or coordinating brains and tongue (language)—is still unknown.

> If you look at the archaeological record, a creative explosion shows up in a narrow window, somewhere between 150,000 and roughly 75,000 years ago. All of a sudden, there's an explosion of complex artifacts, symbolic representation, measurement of celestial events, complex social structures—a burst of creative activity that almost every expert on prehistory assumes must have been connected with the sudden emergence of language. And it doesn't seem to be connected with physical changes; the articulatory and acoustic systems of contemporary humans are not very different from those of 600,000 years ago. There was a rapid cognitive change. Nobody knows why.[27]

An Inconvenient Truth

Though I *am loath to tell* this story of an unfortunate incident that befell yours truly—it seems the peak of Courtney's entire Ecuadorian experience. So I guess I can be big enough to share it ...

During one of those late afternoon lulls that occur between high noon's energy and early evening's revival, when the weaker among us take a nap, I decide to explore the outlying neighborhoods beyond the gringo route. We have lost Carly to the "weaker among us" category, more specifically because she has at long last succumbed to gringatic (my word) intestinal woes. ~~My butt is on fire!~~ She deserts us. But, before she leaves it is decided between the two of them, "We can't let mom go alone." Courtney reluctantly agrees to accompany me. So, with this kind of attitude off we go.

La, la, la, la, la. I'm having great fun exploring the outskirts of the city. But Courtney constantly drags a few paces behind me.

The further we walk from the polished and prospering City Center the more disparity we see between the housing. The neighborhood soon becomes a conglomerate of economic diversity—from the extremely poverty-ridden to the opulent adobe abodes—and everything in between.

Maybe it is the acrid smell of a burning tire that stops me dead in my tracks, but through a fenced enclosure I stumble upon a shockingly impoverished scene. Beside a weathered and dreary shack of nail-exposed wood, looking to be in several stages of collapse, a small group of ragtag, soot-encrusted children (plus a few scrawny chickens and mongrel dog) ramble around an all-dirt yard, unmindful of the black smoke spewing from a burning tire, roiling in their midst. The children's blackened, vacant faces look neither happy nor sad as they busy themselves scraping in the dirt. (The house appears to be parcel to a mechanics garage.) I am stunned speechless by the sight.

Faced with this dismal scene Courtney suggests, "Mom, let's turn around." "Just one more street," I plead. "Look, that street looks really interesting." I spot an opulent, gated-compound with a yellow, two-story mansion, harboring an abundance of lush tropical gardens and terraces.

Hmmmm, boy is this place exceptionally fortified! There's a twenty-foot high, thick adobe fence topped by spiraling razor wire, and security cameras everywhere. *Intriguing.* I wonder what lies behind all this intense fortification. Hey, what luck! I see there is a six inch, round hole in the fancy double gate, just perfect to get a glimpse into their inner sanctum! I place my snoopy face in the perfectly-sized hole only to have unwittingly presented a perfect target, an unexpected gift if you will, for two ferocious attack dogs! (I wonder if a red bull's-eye is painted on the other side.)

I supremely tick-off a pair of now wildly enraged, yowling, charging Rottweilers!

Four feet in the air I jump from a standing position and let out an unintentional primal scream—the kind of scream you're surprised to *hear yourself* make. On the way down, I instinctively clutch at Courtney's arm like a cat falling from a light pole.

Well. This makes Courtney's day. Gales of laughter pour forth from the very depths of her being—flowing right past the several thousand dollars worth of orthodontics we have sunk into her teeth. I *have never seen her* so swept away, so convulsed in hysterics, so delicious with mirth. ALL THE WAY BACK to the hotel instant replays in her head tumble her barely-contained sober countenance into tear-producing laughing fits. She's just *champing at the bit*, just dying to share her rendition with Carly. GLAD I COULD BE SO AMUSING FOR YOU! ' (I can't blame her; I would be laughing too. Where does she get this kind of behavior?)

Why is this story so not fun to write?

Yes, I got my just desserts. I know this. I am chagrinned. But in my sheepish, lame defense (cue Law & Order's "Duh! Duh!" here) I claim *genetic predisposition*: somewhere embedded in the female DNA code is a cozy reading lamp by a window; I'm sure of it. ("Crick! Look at what I

---

*   I haven't seen her laugh nearly this hard since—after boldly announcing my daring intent—I fell down face-first in the snow after an attempted ski jump: instant s*plat and splayed out* just like a cartoon. (Carly laughs uncontrollably at this shared memory as well.) *Of course they made sure I wasn't dead before they burst into sister-bonding hysterics.*

found here!!" shouts Watson.') We like to look *into* the spaces where others live, drawn to the hearth like moths to a flame. Who among those of female persuasion is not intrigued by homes and gardens? (There's a whole magazine devoted to this!) From the excesses of the rich, to the charming, vintage cottage, to the New York loft and Brownstone, to the hovel with a lovingly placed flowering plant, *it's an enjoyable exercise in fantasizing* ... like looking into people's windows at Christmastime—I mean from a car, not like a skulking Peeping Tom. (Quit judging me.)

I come from a long line of snoopy, Sunday afternoon packs of females, loaded into the two-door sedan (you had to push the seat forward and crawl into the back in those days) with possibly a male-coerced-driver forced to cruise aimlessly around with us (our clan never the high-achievers). Through neighborhoods and countryside alike we were all thoroughly entertained by the spectacle of various habitats—dwellings fantasized as sheltering perfect family harmony, domestic bliss and effortless affluence. (Add an ice cream cone or mug of root beer and it was sheer heaven.) Nearing dusk, cozy reading lamps would alight in the windows, bestirring reflections of warmth and security ... probably stemming from deeply buried, ancient memories when our wandering tribal ancestors caught sight of a distant primordial campfire[†]... *blah blah blah.* Courtney's still reeling with laughter, destroying my profound musings.

We stop momentarily so I can make her take a picture of me (if she can contain herself long enough to hold the camera steady) leaning coolly against a graffiti covered wall (photo on cover). Illusory visage of competence, check √. We continue the long walk back to the hotel, me accompanied by intermittent bursts of merciless, pitiless caterwauling.

(And yes, Carly—who could thoroughly relate—was just as intensely amused when she hears the tale.) Oh Hahahahahaahahahahaa.

---

[*] That's Frances Crick and James Watson who co-discovered the DNA spiral molecular structure in 1953.

[†] And yes, cave women wanted to see how the other caves were decorated.

Cañari

Brief Background The Cañari *indígena* are believed to have inhabited this region for several millennia. They were one of the strongest and fiercest peoples ever to successfully resist the formidable legions of invading Incas (1460 AD); nevertheless, they eventually succumbed to the Incan conquerors. The Cañaris had called this region *Guapodeleg* "land as big as heaven"; the Incas renamed it *Tumipampa* (or Tomebamba), "field of axes or knives"; the Spanish conquerors followed in quick succession (by about fifty years) and designated the area *Cuenca* "river basin" after a city in Spain. (Well, actually *Santa Ana de Los Cuatro Ríos de Cuenca* as you know.)

The Incas are thought to have introduced their lingua franca *Quechua* language which transitioned into the regional dialect of *Quichua*. (It's confusing to me to just change the *e* to an *i*.) The Spanish missionaries then took Quichua as a lingua franca to Christianize the populace. And so on and so forth it goes.

Though I said we *intended* to sign up *post haste* for the indigenous day-long immersion, doing so proves to be another matter entirely. Easily locating the cultural main headquarters downtown—a multi-storied, aged complex housing a hodgepodge of indigenous crafts and businesses—it is bewildering to locate the actual office. Though we inquire several times, *no one in the building seems to know where it is!!!?* Finally, after repetitively hitting every shop on every level, we discover a small door (one of several) at ground level. The unlocked door leads to a skylight-illuminated main entrance hall, but *Where is everybody?* No one's answering the ringing phone in the side office, the restaurant doors are shuttered (and we were anxious to sample the native foods so heartily described by our guide book) and there's a note on an office door that says something like, "We are open every other Wednesday." Huh? There's no additional information identifying *which* Wednesday they mean. How do we know when to sign up? We meander around by ourselves for a lengthy period of time (we really want to do this immersion) before someone who seems possessed of some kind of *indígena cred* casually drops in. We immediately spring, restrain him ~~with duct tape~~ and extract what information we can. Our direct inquiries are met with an amorphous, circuitous response about the general probability that this program exists and actually takes place at a certain point in time. (Kind of like quarks.)

Okay then! Here are all our credit cards and we will be back here tomorrow morning!*

Next Morning

Have we been forgotten? Was there a translation misunderstanding (our arrangements are a bit more substantial than my facetious description)? The spacious room in the Mamá Kinua Cultural Center where we await is sparsely decorated with posters, community brochures and children's paintings, which we peruse and peruse until we can't peruse anymore. It's pleasant, but we are getting concerned. *Are we here at the right time, on the right day?* The time drags from our eight a.m. arrival and closes in on 9:30 a.m. Finally, a person of interest (who appears to be some kind of tour spokesman) pokes his head in the door to announce there's *been a delay* but we'll be leaving shortly. Relief.

By 9:45 we are headed out of town in a mud-splashed ATV (all-terrain vehicle), the only passengers driven by a thirtyish Cañari man. We are very soon outside the city on a winding country road, traversing through lovely, grassy, rolling hillside, all sunny, campestral and sparsely populated. There's a most peculiar sight here to grab our attention: the completely incongruous spectacle of American-style homes thus far unseen by us in Ecuador. How puzzling to see the two-story, stucco mini-mansions (most standing isolated within a few acres of land), like any I would encounter in my own city of Yakima (minus the poultry and livestock grazing freely). *What?* Our driver's explanation is that the homes are built from income sent by relatives working in the U.S. and Spain. (In fact, there exists a large community of Ecuadorians in … *Queens, New York!*) Though the homes look quite proper, our guide adds that it is not uncommon for the local inhabitants to house the farm animals *inside* as well.

---

*   An exaggeration of our persistent naïveté.

For the first time we are in need of the ATV when we turn up a rutted dirt road between green pastureland. Within a short distance we come upon the modestly-sized, attractive community building made of mud brick and wood beams. A hand-painted sign in black letters "**Kañari**¹ **ShUNgU**" has been erected above an inviting veranda. We have no idea what to expect as we descend from the vehicle's high steps. Our driver vanishes. For awhile we mill about the open parking lot, admiring some black puppies lolling about in the grass. There's a sagging, deserted volleyball net in the open field and what appears to be a broken zip line—but no visible activity of anybody in sight. So, we wait. And wait.

I retreat and hang out on the shaded veranda bench.

Finally, a subdued clattering sound comes from a small side building. At a leisurely pace, our Cañari hostess emerges with a large wooden breakfast tray in hand. The fortyish *indígena* woman looks *very exotic* to us with long braids, white high-top fedora hat, full green skirt, fuchsia top and overlying black sweater, all covered by a blue-checked, gingham apron. She makes a speechless offering of food and, through head gestures, invites us to follow her inside the community building. We find the cool, dark interior to be of a hard-pack, earthen floor, furnished with rudimentary wood benches and chairs. Once seated, we are presented—in simple, handmade, brown clay bowls and cups with wooden spoons—their traditional foods of maize, eggs, bread, sweet té (tea), and ... CANE ALCOHOL! In an oblique glance, I see that our hostess—gentle, regal and mild-mannered—instantly bottoms-up and slams down her alcohol portion! Brain scramble! *What do I do?* I am in *their culture*; would it be dreadfully rude to refuse to partake, like declining to drink goat's blood with a sub-Saharan tribe? † *Under her steady watchful gaze*, though I have not drunk alcohol in years, I acquiesce.

---

* I encounter an exasperating moving target whenever trying to determine the correct spelling of Native Amerindian words (e.g. Kañari, Cañari)—I presume because many of the languages were never originally written. For example: Inka or Inca; Quichua or Kichwa; Cusco or Cuzco or Q'osco; huaca or waka; rendering me coo-coo, koo-koo or qoo-qoo.

† According to Judy Blackenship's book *Cañar* it seems I was right to accept the alcohol offering; a refusal can be insulting. Though I wondered about my "goat's blood" analogy, she tells of a similar sharing and drinking of a freshly slaughtered cow's blood (with a dash of liquor) preceding a Kañari *fiesta de carnival.*²⁸

OOOOOOOHHHHH—WHEEEEEEEE PACHAMAMA! THIS STUFF IS STRONG! I figure the girls will be just as politely, politically-correct come their turn, as a savvy observance of the host culture, only to see them simply push their high-proof drink aside. *What?* It's not long after I am feeling woozy—and have to step outside for some fresh air.

What was I thinking? … well <u>nothing</u> anymore!!! La la la, would you look at all that bucolic countryside, dappled in sunlight …

Returning inside and after enjoying what I can best describe as hominy grits—and I like this kind of food—our guide for the day appears. *Alfonso* is a middle-aged Cañari man, small in stature, dressed in Western clothes save the *indígena típica* black Fedora hat. We feel fortunate to be his sole participants for the day as he explains the day's agenda in Spanish. We are to follow him for a walk through his ancestral land, partake of *a Pampamesa* traditional foods lunch (*Pampamesa* literally translates as table or *mesa* in the field or *pampa*) and then return to the center for an authentic display of music, craft and dance.

Climbing a hill directly adjacent to the communal hut, we follow him up a winding path. I'm staring down at his thick-soled, black rubber shoes as he leads in a strong measured pace. Soon we are submerged within a brushy, foliage area consisting of valued native plants. As we walk the path, he pauses to point out their medicinal uses, plants traditionally used by his people for maladies such as stress, childbirth, back pain, cramps etc., all marked for identification by wood post signage. I am paying close attention, but with the unfamiliarity of the Spanish and Quichua languages (and confusing names like *Iguila Jabon* and *Wikundo Grmelia*) it is a great strain to retain much of any imparted botanical knowledge. (Carly—justifiably—gets crabby if I ask her to translate too much.) The one medicinal plant I do retain, however, because it is *oh so relevant*, is the one intended to ease the pain of childbirth. Although I respect our soft-spoken man-guide, Alfonso laments about how too many of the women are now going to modern facilities for childbirth and not following the ancestral ways, saying, "Women have been having babies for thousands of years, but now they are going to the clinic more and more!" I had to wonder … how many HELL-ON-EARTH childbirths had Alfonso experienced? (Two were accompanying me.)

Before long, we reach the top of the hill where we find a traditional Cañari gathering place. It is a grassy, partially-open area with a smattering of trees, but mostly a continuance of the green, brushy vegetation. At this point we are invited to participate in a ceremony for Pachamama or Mother Earth.

We stand behind Alfonso in quiet reverence, and follow his lead.

First, we face east toward the origin of sunrise. We all take a deep breath, place palms out and extend both arms as Alfonso projects in a soft, sonorous voice, the intention:

"To get energy for our Mother Earth Pachamama, for the plants, animals, and people."

The ceremony proceeds, following an east, north, west and south orientation accompanied by Alfonso's oratory:

Este: Breathe in—exhale.
"Thank you for the energy for Estados Unidos [United States] for our visiting friends."

Norte: Breathe in—exhale.
"Thank you for the energy for the plants."

Oeste: Breathe in—exhale.
"Thank you for the energy from our setting sun."

Sud: Breathe in—exhale.
"Thank you for the energy to the Incas in the south and our friends in Peru."

After this we are given a *lonnnnnggg* period for meditation, nearly an hour or so, "to feel the energy of Mother Earth."[*] We each retreat to our respective

---

* However reluctant I am to break the spell, it did not go without notice that when Alfonso fell into a deep meditative state, a sacred chant reverberated from him that sounded suspiciously like snoring. (*Does that count?*) We exchanged puzzled glances.

positions: Alfonso reclines next to a log while we sit some distance away from him and from one another.

At the end of this contemplative time, he asks that we take with us "the energy and respect for the earth— especially in concern for the depletion of the ozone layer and global warming."

Then we continue our trek down the other side of the hill.

The Awe-Inspiring Inca

For me, the prospect of setting foot again on any part of an Incan road is thrilling. From all I had read—stimulated from our 2005 travels in Peru—I never dreamed I would have another opportunity. But here I am. The main *Qhapaq ñan* is the *Great Road or grand central route* connecting the northern and southern borders of the 15th century Incan Empire, all passing through Cuzco Peru, the heart and royal command center. The ingenious, strategic road system facilitated Incan control over an extraordinarily expansive empire. Within less than one hundred years, the Incas (the original use of the word *Inca,* meaning *children of the sun,* attributed only the supreme rulers, not the people) had amassed a realm extending over 2,500 miles along the continent, including what are now portions of Ecuador (plus a small edge of Colombia), Bolivia, Chile and Argentina. Such an efficiently controlled kingdom and massive road system is comparable to a reign the expanse of the United States from the east coast to west coast, or from Washington State to somewhere in Mexico, north to south. No Amerindian empire in the Western Hemisphere has matched their spectacular achievements. Tumipampa (now Cuenca) was established as part of their northern kingdom by the Inca Tupac-Yupanqui in 1490 AD. (And is a contender for the possible location of the fabled "El Dorado" city of gold.) Alas, Tumipampa was to be short-lived: in less than fifty years the entire Incan reign succumbed to the advancing Spaniards.[*]

On this green hill of conifers, overlooking the distant valley of Cuenca, seven-foot tall plumes of cream-colored pampas grass line the red-soiled, earth road like standing sentinels. It is strikingly beautiful. Stepping on the Incan path is a special moment for me, as I imagine the legions of Incans who tread this same ground over five centuries ago en route to build their northernmost kingdom.[†]

---

[*] Contributing factors to this rapid coup d'état were that the Incas themselves were embroiled in a civil war—led by two warring brothers—and the devastating toll of European diseases.

[†] My rose-colored glasses of history do not encompass what was by all accounts a bloody takeover.

The exposed rock and soil on this hillside consists of strange and surreal colors: swirls of distinctive yellow ochre and terra cotta with tinges of rose and corral pink … like nothing I had ever seen before. The red-earth soil beneath my feet splashes with luminous golden ochre. Turbulent overcast skies, dark and threatening, make the mineral colors all the more vivid. Alfonso tells us that this unique convergence of natural beauty is considered sacred ground to his people and the site of special Cañar gatherings twice a year, propitiating the mountain spirits with music and fire. I can only imagine the extraordinary scene.

I ask for permission to take a small rock; he approves with a nod.

As we are left to explore, Alfonso pulls a wooden flute from his satchel and plays a melody. The solo is hauntingly beautiful, resonant in this hallowed space.

Back up to the top of the hill we go, where we are to await our luncheon. Again, this turns into a cosmic lesson for patience-challenged European-Westerners like us: try with all our might, our minds cannot inhabit the same space-time continuum as many Amerindians. "Unlike us, they understand that part of enjoying any local event is the hours of patient waiting and watching."[29] (Blackenship) From what I understand, it is a *típica* Cañar characteristic to observe the passing of time with a great deal of laxity: it is subjective and malleable.

As before, Alfonso lies down and lounges in the grass, as we three separate from each other and attempt to engage in solitary spiritual-awakening. *What a wonderful opportunity!* I think. We sit cross-legged, meditate and commune with nature—a disciplined resolve that lasts about eight minutes. We are done. Thereafter ensues a test of endurance: we are *really hungry* now but must wait interminably for our lunch to appear. *A lonnngggggg* time passes. *Were we supposed to conjure it up with our energy thoughts?* Occasionally I engage one eye to peer over my shoulder at Alfonso; hat cocked over his eyes, he is a vision of quiet, calm repose.

Hard as I try I am so *truly ashamed* to admit that during this great expanse of time, my mind kept wandering back to all those adrenalin-inducing, unexplored, rainbow-colored craft shops back in the city! They beckon to me like crack cocaine (I imagine) while we are lolling our finite time away here in the grass! What's wrong with me? *Am I so shallow?* Though I am, admittedly, bitten by mere mortal, flesh-weak shopping fever, Courtney's flesh is actually being bitten by *muchos insectos*. Pachamama's mosquito minions are having their way with her. Big time! (Carly and I have not a problem whatsoever, of course.) Should I happen, unintentionally, to glance her way, I am met with the pitiful expression of a puppy pleading to go outside: *Pleeeeeeeeaaaasssse, oh please, when can we leave!!!!?* she begs with her eyes.

At long last a white fedora hat can be seen bobbing up the climbing trail. Can it be??? The hat is soon followed by the rest of our Cañari hostess emerging from the brush, carrying cloth-covered baskets of food and accompanied by her twelve-year-old son.

Our Pampamesa feast can finally begin! A grassy spot is chosen to lay a long and narrow white cloth on the ground—perhaps seven by three feet. After we are seated around the perimeter, each food offering is poured in ritualistic order from a basket or other warming container, along the center of the blanket. Alfonso lends a hand to help the woman and her son with the food presentation, speeding up the process. (Carly's ravenous thought: *JUST POUR IT allllll ouuuuutttttttttt!!!!*) A colorful ensemble of maize, potatoes, lentils, cauliflower, carrots, and rice emerges from the containers plus several bowls of hot sauce and a very sweet beverage of *té* (tea), derived from various local plants. We are each issued a large wooden spoon with which we are to communally partake of the spread. Once completed, Alfonso sits at the head of the ... blanket and proceeds to offer gratitude to Pachamama for our food. We gingerly lift our spoons, apprehensive and keen to follow the lead of our hosts in such an unfamiliar setting. (*Dear Abby, when seated around a blanket of food with Cañari indígenas ...*) Alfonso digs in with gusto, completely unabashed. *Okay then, let's go!*

Nevertheless, I still have no idea where, or if, I am supposed to honor some kind of imperceptible food boundary; nothing whatsoever delineates a personal property-restrictive zone. Though I feel awkward, and therefore delicately proceed, I soon notice the boy has no compunction whatsoever about drifting over into my immediate territory to snatch a golden potato I had my eye on; thereafter, I *try* to loosen up and eat with as much gusto as I can muster. Vegetarian Carly, thrilled by this beautiful bounty of vegetables, proves the most adept at vigorous consumption. (Courtney comment later: "Geez Carly, you practically ate the whole blanket.")

The Cañari woman, Mariana, and her son, Manuel, are so mild-mannered and soft spoken that the boy will *only whisper* into his mother's ear and never attempts to engage in direct communication with any of us. (Cañari children are known to be excessively shy.) He is attired in a smart, dark gray, team jacket, black jeans, and knit stocking cap. After awhile, his incessant whispering seems a bit strange *to us,* though we are the recipients of a few pleasant smiles. It is clear, however, that he and his mother enjoy an admirable and affectionate rapport. Through Carly's Spanish, we share a moment of good humor when Carly declares mosquito-ravished Courtney to be our *"oferta de carne dulce blanca"* (offering of sweet white meat) to Pachamama. Courtney smiles gamely at our light and easy laughter at her expense.

Call us gastronomical cowards if you will, but to avoid the prospect of the typical roasted guinea pig (*cuy*) or any other *unfamiliar* flesh parts, we indicated ahead of time that we were all vegetarians. This proves an excellent decision as our legume offerings are absolutely delectable: an abundance of warm, exquisitely seasoned, healthy bounty from the land. We are very happy campers. Next to Carly, Alfonso appears the most voracious eater, quickly filling wood spoon after wood spoon with rice, potatoes and maize. Because I cannot speak Quichua or Spanish, I attempt to communicate to Marianna *in smiles* our most sincere enjoyment and appreciation of such a beautifully prepared feast.

Once all are satiated, the remaining food is simply rolled up into the cloth, ready to be transported back home. (Carrying food in cloth is a common Cañari practice.*)

We are then to *spend time digesting our food* ...

---

*   I recently observed a TV spot about an eco-friendly American family *wrapping their children's school lunches in cloth*, very similar to the Cañar age-old practice.

At the end of the digesting period we engage in a lovely ceremony using sweet grass to disperse our individual energies from Pachamama's sacred ground. Standing with arms extended out to each side, Marianna slowly cleanses each of us in turn by waving smoking sweet grass in the immediate vicinity of our bodily energies. Lastly, and with a sense of honor, Carly is chosen to waft sweet smoke around Mariana: above, below, before and behind: all our lingering spiritual residues are vanquished from Pachamama's sacred earth.

When we initially began our trek we had observed three teenagers orienting a huge cumbersome TV antenna on a hillock just above the Kañari community hut. When we returned they were still finagling with the antennae. Courtney observes: "Dad would have us doing that all day, too, if it meant watching a football game."

Last but not least, we return to the community hall for demonstrations of traditional native crafts. First, a lesson in spinning wool by our hostess. This involves taking a clump of llama wool on-a-stick (looking like a cotton candy) with the extended part of the stick held under the left arm. Her left-hand's supple fingers are placed at the bottom of the white clump, streaming and twisting the hair into a single strand, meeting the lower right-hand fingers, also deftly maneuvering the strand, while twirling and spinning onto a drop spindle. The unprocessed clump magically becomes spun yarn before our very eyes! This skilled craftsmanship involves a dexterity I couldn't possibly hope to emulate (i.e., I try my hand and am hopeless. However, I do try to project *intelligent curiosity* with my facial expressions.) Then comes a chance to pummel maize on a flat grinding stone. With relief, we eagerly embrace a more rudimentary task and stampede toward the hefty (two by one foot) stone. Once I brush the girls aside for my turn, an oblong rock is used like a rolling pin to crush the kernels, reducing them to white flour. I find the crack and pummeling of the rolled grain to be quite gratifying!

Alfonso reappears with a guitar in hand and attired in the more traditional garb of a bright red poncho. He proceeds to treat the three of us to a guitar strumming musical performance. Unfortunately, for the rollicking children we had just seen happily playing outside, they are soon *compelled* to join in the performance, adding a drum and a *guayo* (scraping musical thing) to the mix. Responding to Alfonso's sharp commands, we feel sorry for the kids (and a bit uncomfortable) by the clearly pained expression on their faces, as if they are forced to sing (an exceptionally anguished look on the lone girl among the four boys). However, once the dancing portion begins, and we are pulled into a circle of revelry with them, the children come alive with the addition of *our compelled* participation. It truly does unlock a feeling of camaraderie, of shared exuberance, as we spin in a circle of clasped hands.

It is around four p.m. when we head back once again in the ATV. (Carly, with foreboding intestinal rumblings, her thoughts consumed by the threat of bodily retribution for having eaten with such wild abandon: "I'm gonna pay for having eaten that blanket, " she whimpers.)

Whirling down the hillside, nearing town, we come upon, what is to us, a most peculiar sight: large stereo speakers mounted on a pick-up truck, blasting a sorrowful religious dirge. Behind the creeping truck, several men carry a litter transporting a glass-encased ceramic statue of a saint; the statue is diminutive, ornate and gold. Behind the truck, a small walking procession of mostly mestizo women, somberly scatter flower petals. This tiny demonstration is preceded by an officially brusque police escort. I crane my neck to take it all in, but the music swiftly dissipates into the distance as we careen forward.

That evening, we are relaxing in our hotel room, soothed by the familiarity of having a TV on just like at home, when suddenly on the evening news, an alarmed newscaster anxiously reports an armed robbery! Our combined attention focuses on the agitated, serious-toned broadcast. Spanish Babble … Spanish Babble … Spanish Babble (to me) cut to shot of the PLAZA DE SAN FRANCISCO DE CUENCA—**HEY THAT'S OUR PLAZA, THE ONE RIGHT OUTSIDE OUR WINDOW!** Six widened-eyes meet each other; Carly confirms what Courtney and I suspect! A collective, heightened anxiety surges between us—and then, just as rapidly drops down to a shoulder shrug—what can we possibly do about it now?[*]

A peculiarity: I was puzzled by a pair of white *chonis* (chō knees or underwear) lying in the street just outside our hotel for our entire stay. No one ever bothered to pick them up? *Why doesn't someone pick them up?*

---

[*]   I often shudder at the thought of where we might *naively* be staying, considering the locations of some of our hotels at home.

Turning the Tables

Sometimes I try to imagine what it would be like to have daily, back-to-back busloads of *indígenas* eager to photograph and observe *my every move* ...

My evening walk becomes of intense interest as I am being watched and covertly photographed by groups of Amerindians, ogling me, but projecting an air of nonchalance whenever I look their way—then quickly brandish a camera the instant I look off. They take a keen interest in my most mundane of activities, including the clothes I'm wearing. Heads turn in discernment as I reach my usual spot (in approximately 1.5 miles) encircle it, and return home. (Yes, I have to circle it.)

Possible Perplexities [PP] of the South American natives: *What useless, strange behavior? She's not even chewing coca leaves on her journey to give her energy or to tell how far she has gone* (though you can be pretty sure ~~I would if I could~~ I've got plenty of caffeine in my system). *Hmmmm, no neighbor visited, no chicken or guinea pig acquired for the evening pot, no sacred offering made to Mother Earth. And how can we tell what village she belongs to when everyone's clothing looks so alike? That "Blue Pants Tribe" must be the most prodigious!* (a)

Why are so many of these villagers walking and running so fast with no apparent destination, plugging their ears with little machines? They are blocking out all the wind and mountain spirits! Perhaps the fastest ones are delivering an urgent message to the next village, much like our Inca chasquis did! (b)

Moving on to a community park, the group stands transfixed around a most bizarre spectacle.

PP: *What is the meaning of all those locals circling around and around and around ... perhaps it's a sacred circle, honoring their Nike and Adidas gods (the symbols most often seen stitched all over their clothes and shoes)? Yes, it must be for a spiritual ritual!*

---

*   In some areas coca chewing can relate to estimated distances, i.e., four wads of chew and walk to get there.

†   Long distance messenger/runners dispersed across the vast Incan empire.

(a) jeans (b) joggers (c) a running track

209

They have even built indoor circles for this! Let's start a fire in the center for them in a show of honor to their gods! We will leave our finest coca leaves and a sacrificial llama fetus. They will thank us! (c)

A tour bus full of derby-hatted Quechuas pulls up to the window of a fitness club; their shocked and quizzical faces peer out from all the bus windows. Flashes from cameras explode at the rows and rows of people going nowhere on treadmills and stationary bikes, the entire panting group dominated by a muscular overseer.

PP: "Are these human-slave-powered machines grinding grain or pumping water somewhere unseen beneath the floor?" they query the tour guide. Many pondering: *Shouldn't someone tell the bicyclers they are not going anywhere—or at least have the courtesy to put the wheels back on for them? What a cruel society to trick them so! And how can they still be so fat? They must be fed a lot of grains! Perhaps they're preparing them, warming them up, for a sacred royal feast.*

The bus pulls forward to the next window.

PP: *This is a very strange sight. What powers does that strong woman leader hold over her agonizing, convoluted subjects, straining to imitate her every move? And what horrific fate befalls those who fail to mimic her? Perhaps for a punishment, they're placed on those cruel bicycles that go nowhere?* En masse the group rushes over to render assistance to the anguished contortionists: "let's all help them to get straightened out!" (d)

A wandering group of *Aymaras* have drifted into my neighborhood, hoping to get a close-up view of real-life inhabitants in their native dwellings—and feeling lucky to be catching the moment when I am laboriously harvesting a crop before their very eyes! One that has been meticulously watered, fertilized and nurtured—then cut, gathered and stored in a large, black bag. (e)

PP: *That green plant must be very valuable for so much work! Do the women grind it to put in soup or a make a delicious fermented brew like our chicha (ccusa) beer?*

---

*   (d) yoga class (e) I mow the lawn

Or perhaps they use it to make wonderful weaving creations—like hats, sweaters and blankets— as we do? (I could try; hand me a glue gun.) *Maybe they take their harvest to Saturday market to sell* (I could try …). *All that effort and spent resources must produce something of great value!*

Toward evening, peering out my living room curtains, I see that hordes of Amerindians are lingering about the sidewalks, trying to get a glimpse into my windows, eager so see how my daily life is conducted. And for a fee I let them in!

Home Tour: Coin changer around my belly, I say with a sweeping hand motion worthy of Vanna White: "Over here you can see the household man watching TV after a hard day's work. No, there is no particular sports season he is watching; they all run together in our culture now— one after the other, flowing into one continuous, high-profit stream. The sports competitions and their play-offs are never over, stretching into infinity …" I say with a far off look in my eye and hint of resentment. "Follow me into the kitchen where I will demonstrate how I prepare the evening meal. (Use of a bullhorn here) This is a can and a can opener. Now move aside so those in the back can see. I am using the can opener just as my ancestors taught me; I am proud to say I now use a manual one in order to save energy for the planet. Would anyone like to try it? Make a straight line please," I plead as they charge forward en masse. "Don't worry, you'll all get a chance for a picture to show the folks back home; remember there's an extra charge if I'm in it!"

"So where-y'all from? Riobamba? Abra Huashuaccasa? Huancavelica? Quentatocaxtahl? Good people there!"

Continuing (after everyone has had a chance to turn the can opener) …

"Usually, after eating dinner of a typical American diet like say, oh, spaghetti, tacos or stir-fry, we have quality time staring at some kind of screen, all apart from one another. See, there's my daughter now in the computer room. Don't you dare slam that door again missy! I told you it's a tour! It may help fund your college education! … Now where was I?" (I resume my placid smile.) "Oh yeah, infrequently I sit with the household man and try to coax him to walk in outdoor circles with me. Normally, he flatly refuses."

211

"Later—if you're still lurking about when it's dark—you'll notice that nearly every single household in our neighborhood is all locked up tight and pulsating with a blue television light! In olden days people used to spend time together visiting, kids even played outdoors. Notice all those empty front porch chairs? No one has ever been seen sitting in one! Be sure to take a photo if you catch someone! It is rare. The chairs are mostly props, solely for decoration. The indoor children are now consumed with "cyberspace." Don't ask me what that is."

"The next day we repeat everything again, exactly the same way. Are there any questions?"

I hear them whispering an observation: (This next comment taken from a true story.)

"We noticed you have bathrooms INSIDE THE HOUSE! Sometimes even near where you eat! We find this disgusting!" they decry. "At least we have the sense to go away from where we live!"

—"I kinda think the neighbors wouldn't like that," I defensively retort.

"Are those round metal sculptures we see on so many rooftops like *Toros*—an homage to Mother Earth to bless the house? Or perhaps the round disk is to capture and honor the sacred light of father Sun God?"

—"No, those are satellite dishes, in homage to, uh, Hollywood's gods and goddesses, our sacred stars."

"Why does everyone have such large houses for only a few people? Even computers and cars have their own rooms! Where are the elders and the cousins and the rest of the clan?"

—"Uh, we don't like any of those people. We're dysfunctional enough as it is for a nuclear family."

"How come your neighbors seem to shun you by hiding inside their locked homes and cars?"

—"I take great umbrage to that! We shun them too!"

"Why are the vast majority of houses and businesses painted dull shades of beige, brown, gray or white? Are the uses of beautiful bold colors outlawed or some kind of cultural taboo?"

—"Yeah, kind of … don't you guys have any pueblo covenants? "

Next, I take them to a typical large chain grocery store where they find reams and reams of other-worldly colored foods, many concealed from view in plastic packaging and tin cans.

"How do you know where this stranger-food comes from and that it is good for you?" someone asks.

—"We trust that the faceless giant corporations who produce our food are noble and trustworthy when it comes to concerns for our health (while strongly suspecting that they don't give a rat's ass about us and would probably put one [a rat's ass] in our food if they could get away with it and it turned a profit)." I'm beginning to question our cultural sanity.

"In the face of such abundance, why do most shoppers look so sour (like they were weaned on a pickle or a jalepeño)? Very few seem friendly or engaged in lively social exchange like we do on our market days?" Just then an adult slovenly shopper walks by, clad in flannel pajamas and fluffy bedroom slippers, searching for a diet Cola. To my gawking tour group I have no reasonable explanation for this current trend.

"Please explain, what is 'Diet Food?'"

—"Diet foods are those that provide less calorie energy for more money. Usually they taste horrible."

(They cannot grasp this concept whatsoever.)

But nothing is as shocking as the entire row of our super-indulgent pet food section. What a concept! Entire industries competing for the taste buds of dogs, cats, birds, gerbils—and even vermin like rats!

"Do Americans have no food scraps? Is that why they're so fat?" Camera flashes light up the entire aisle, momentarily blinding the elderly patron reaching for her canary seed. Close-ups are taken of the most absurd items like: *rubber* bones, Halloween holiday outfits, elaborate beds, fake tree limbs (climbing pedestals), *low-fat diet foods,* special shampoos, pet vitamins in gravy sauce and teething toys. "No one back home will ever believe us without photos!"

At the end of the day, I seriously question who has the stranger culture.

Sadly, The Last Day

Clang clang clangclangclang, clang clang clang clang. The church bell rings erratic enough you know a fallible human being is ringing it. One, two, three, four, five, six, seven. It must be seven a.m. Courtney pulls a pillow over her ears and threatens to ring the bell-clanger senseless if he doesn't stop: "I'd go to church just to kill him," she proclaims.

We have found it to be essential to settle into one place for a minimum of three days in order to give the brain time enough to adjust, get its bearings, and to feel comfortable in its new surroundings (the brain loves consistency). Thereafter manifests the pleasure of returning to *known* spots, those we have heroically discovered and can now return to with recognizable ease (i.e., we beat it back to Café Austria again).

This third-day morning the café is filled with an assortment of characters, mostly Europeans attired in neck-wrapped scarves draped over worn, woolen sweaters (looking ever so stylish *as only they can*). I can hear French, Italian and possibly Dutch spoken. One twenty-something couple looks as though they stepped right out of a fashion magazine photo shoot for beautiful global backpackers. He is dark-haired handsome, with curly-locks of hair, and sporting a scruffy days-growth beard. His female companion is delicate chic blonde and model pretty. They look fashionably rumpled with their maps and compass and backpacks strewn on the table.

We linger over our coffees and pastries while perusing newspapers or writing in journals (since this place is *ours* now we feel free to linger like locals). Courtney snaps a photo of me in the process of writing, and, though Carly sits right next to me, cuts her entirely out of the picture. Carly protests, "Hey!" and Courtney quips, "Writers are lonely people … … *Snaggle*." Ding, ding, ding, let the rounds begin.

We briefly assess our dwindling financial state, to wit Courtney pointedly interjects, "If we had *just sat* in Puerto López, we would've saved a lot of money." (As opposed to taking boat tours, hike tours, horse rides, etc.)

Well technically *that's true, but* …?

As I am earnestly writing notes in my journal, Courtney—equal parts bored and annoyed—out of the clear blue, reaches over to purposely smack the top of my pencil, creating a deep harsh scribble on my paper. This gets my attention.

WHERE DOES SHE GET THIS TYPE OF HUMOR!? THIS STARTLE-FUNNY BEHAVIOR? (It is amusing ...)[*]

Today the streets are abuzz with festivities. It is the kick-off for the celebration of the ***Bicentenario de Ecuador*** or 200 year independence from Spain. Everywhere we turn there is live music, a dance production or some sort of entertainment. I am in heaven. Several well-choreographed groups of dancers in ethnic regalia take to the main plaza in display of traditional dance; their styles reflective of Spanish origins and/or those of several distinct native cultures. Throw into this mix the *cholos cuencanos,* a dancing troupe representing **a blend** of *Inca, Cañari and Spanish* blood, and I am in a whirl! Wow, this is so cool. Many of the costumes of the dancers so colorful, bizarre, and nearly surreal, I can't possibly begin to describe them. I am standing in a crowd of at least two hundred people taking in the performances of foot stomping men, women's voluminous skirts flaring, all of them twirling and yipping in circles to a live Andean band. My heart inadvertently leaps with the surprise *shout and toss* of hats high into the air at the end of one dance extravaganza—I have no idea why it thrilled me so.

We follow the drift of music from one plaza to another, enjoy the bonhomie in the air, the spectacle of families—babies-in-strollers, partaking of all the fine weather opportunities the day has to offer. Colorful cotton candy vendors and balloon makers roam about the streets; sky blue and rainbow-colored flags billow in the wind, promoting the official rainbow flag of indigenous pride.

---

[*] Another example: I am trying to impart my newly-acquired knowledge of cosmic consciousness, peace and harmony to Courtney by drawing a spiral, simulating the expanding energy frequency of good thoughts radiating outward to the universe. Courtney takes the pencil from my hand and scratches a severe 'X" right through the forefront of my spiraling good thoughts. So much for that.

At long last, overwhelming hunger intervenes (I hate this) and we are forced to break for dinner. (Courtney recalls how unusually, *unnaturally happy* I was at the time!) We regroup and repair to our usual restaurant for food—cheese sandwiches and french fries. *Raymipama* is unbelievably packed! By the time we are out of there, it is starting to get dark.

The Odd Observation That Day

* I do not understand the fashion choice by many of the modern female population opting to wear tight tight tight clothes like teeny-tiny cut-offs, skirts or jeans with high spiked heels? And there's the ever ubiquitous popularity of striped Adidas sweat suits. I don't get it.

* Street and plaza names are sometimes *calendar dates*, like the "10 of August Plaza" or the "3rd of November Street." This practice found all over South America, the date indicative of a momentous occasion. (I.e., not just any old date!)

* I notice the prevalence, once again, of the spiky, upturned nails, embedded in the window ledges of ... *a kindergarten*. Is this to keep: loiterers from sitting; criminals from entering; pigeons from pooping; or the children from escaping?

La maesta (teacher) momentarily turns her back to the class. "Agggghhhhh!!!" echoes through the classroom.

La maestra phoning: "¡Señora Sanchez you must come and extract Pablo from the window sill again! I don't know how many times I have warned him not to try and escape no matter how much he hates *matemáticas!* And please make sure all his shots are up-to-date!"'

With dusk upon us, a large screen set up in the main plaza projects a historical retrospective. I contently view the landscape images of

---

* An odd observation here in the states: A recent guest of ours from South America (and just learning English) comments on the *alarming severity* of our "DEAD END" road signs. Translated in Spanish the words are, "FIN DE MUERTO!" Yeah, I guess that is pretty harsh. I certainly wouldn't want to go down that road!

honey-ochre hills (looking much like the hills around Yakima) to green mountain forests highlighting the flora and fauna of their homeland. Of course, I cannot follow the accompanying historical text, intermittently flashed on the screen in Spanish —and I had already used up Carly's translating tolerance for the day—but I'm sufficiently literate enough to get the gist of *Bicentenario* followed by *Simón Bolívar*. (Truth be known, I dared solicit Carly one last time, who ~~snapped~~ tersely summarized: "It's about the history of the bicentennial celebration!!!" And I knew to press no more.) Apparently the movement *toward* liberation began in 1809, the fait accompli led by Simón Bolívar in 1822. Hence the 1809-2009 celebration.

A master of ceremonies appears, fronting a seven-piece band. We are all on ground level; there is no elevated stage. He proceeds to entertain with a fire show accompanied by drumming. Juggled torches are tossed high in the air and then through hoops to a waiting partner. The sight is very dramatic and thrilling against the darkening sky. I observe with interest his female accompanist, possessed of wildly-dyed, pink-red hair that has obliterated her natural dark brown locks; this alternative look seems so out-of-place here. The gathering crowd keeps inching closer and closer to the juggling act when suddenly he pauses. He walks over toward the pressing crowd, sweeps his torch across a wide swathe of asphalt, and lights it afire. Along with the *va voooomth* sound of the exploding ball of gas an audible gasp arises from the crowd. *Everyone backs off.* (I guess that's one means of effective crowd control.)

With his reclaimed space, he proceeds to dazzle with an impressive display of Fire Poi: dual, fire lit balls, tethered to a cord at each end, the length swung concurrently with each hand, above the head and below the feet, in front or behind the back, and crisscrossing every which way to form exquisite geometric patterns. The overall affect is an aesthetic marvel of coordination, tinged with danger, exciting to behold: a mesmerizing illusion as though harnessing small comets stolen from the night sky. (Poi originated in New Zealand and is a Māori word for "ball on a cord.") It seems the practitioners of Poi have become a worldwide phenomenon the likes of which Carly had just witnessed on the beaches of Italy in a fiery display given by a backpacking girl from Ireland. (If you want to see some thrilling examples of fire poi, look up the "Burning Man" festival in Nevada.)

It is getting dark—really dark; the crowds grow as does the alcohol consumption. We decide it is time for all good gringas to go home. *Buenas noches* band leader, *buenas noches* congas and bombas and maracas, *buenas noches* trumpets and flutes (*quenas*) and panpipes (*zampoñas*) and all that I love!

According to the ancient Romans, the Hour of the Wolf means the time between night and dawn, just before the light comes, and people believed it to be the time when demons had a heightened power and vitality, the hour when most people died and most children were born, and when nightmares came to one."[30]

Sound asleep in the nether hours of waning night, it is the Hour of the Wolf when only the baker, the street cleaner and *malo espritus* roam empty streets.

Cascading drum rolls EXPLODE like gunshots throughout our bedroom. *What the?* All of us hope the disturbance will just pass and we can return to our deep slumber. But the intrusive drumming only intensifies. Soon thereafter, the rich baritone of an inebriated soloist wafts up to our second floor balcony through our open shutters; his melodious voice echoes off the empty stone streets below. There is a yearning, romantic tinge to his Spanish love song.

Though reluctant to sacrifice deep beauty rest, I rise to the occasion, resolved not to miss out on a most unique spectacle (I see both girls cover their heads with pillows). How often does one get to hear a romantic lothario crooning in the middle of the night? Stepping out onto the balcony I find the previous evening's master of ceremonies leading an eclectic group of women, children and men—no more than twelve people. The singer is part of a trio of wavering, dark-haired men, engaged in a swaying and listing camaraderie. They are all in a march through the city in what seems to be a continuance of the Independence Day celebration from the night before.

Lingering for a while at the far end of the plaza, the drum-armed group lacks any concern whatsoever for sleeping souls, the loud percussion continues in bombastic, sporadic outbursts, and bounces off the brick plaza and the multi-storied stone buildings. In the dim gray light, I find it hard to discern just what's going on; occasionally there's huddled conversation between the drum leader and his ragtag consortium. After an odd, disjointed gap, the drumming procession lurches on, children straggle alongside, passing beneath our hotel window, then disappear down a dark corridor.

To where I couldn't possibly know.

First steps toward home: Flight to Quito

Yes, it is here I live to dearly regret the missed opportunity of four extra days, lost by my indecisive self when we initially purchased our Ecuador travel tickets so many moons ago. Sadly, I take one long last look around our elegant hotel lobby, its warm wood saturated and glowing in morning light.

I'm not ready to go home; I want to stay.

Our short flight from Cuenca to Quito leaves us in Quito with several hours to kill before our international flight leaves for home at nine p.m.

Can we do it? Can we pack in one last excursion? Old Town Quito (*Casco Colonial*) is a highly recommended destination, but it is a *cross-town* drive from the airport through horrifically congested traffic. (Quito is Ecuador's second largest city of over 1.5 million people.) Do we have adequate time? The taxi driver we hail assures us that, though it may be cutting it close, *he can accomplish this task for us!*

Yikes, here we go again, screaming through what appears to be rush-hour traffic; we are all tense and all watching the clock; it's around 3:45 p.m.

Though the drive is nerve-racking, the Old Town district does not disappoint. Because the densely-packed *Centro Histórico* (historical center) is full of cars and pedestrians, we are dropped some blocks away, making it necessary to walk one marvelously hilly street after another. The streets reveal smart restaurants, cafés, galleries, shops and PEOPLE: MASSIVE AMOUNTS OF PEOPLE migrating en masse up one street and down the other. Where are they all going? What's going on? The nearer we get to the renowned Plaza Grande (*Plaza de la Independencia*) the crowd thickens. Off in the distance we hear the rumbling and roar of multitudes, the unseen pounding of drums. In the midst of such a tremendous assemblage of excitable people I feel a *hair-prickling* transfer of electricity, a visceral current that sweeps over and through my body. I don't know why or what this is; those drumbeats reverberating off the massive stone and that *supernatural collective roar* from a crowd carries some kind of primal power all its own.

221

Dorothy E. Groszhans

Upon entering the majestic, open-air plaza an immense crowd faces a stair-step landing beneath a colonnaded building. From the landing emanates an amplified production of an event upon which everyone is focused, but the content is indecipherable from our distance. It appears to be part of the ongoing Bicentennial Celebration we just left in Cuenca.* I look up at the towering hillsides surrounding Old Town to see the historic date "2009" emblazoned in lights across a mountainside. We have barely two hours of daylight to peruse the architectural, colonial grandeur of this magnificent setting: its spectacular skyscraping statues, colossal museums, Presidential palace, glowing towers and exquisite Cathedrals. Perched on a prominent hill over all, is an ever-present, hovering statue that seems to follow us everywhere: the winged *Virgin of the Americas*. (Another virgin of course.)

We do our best to appreciate utter magnificence in our limited time. But, how can you take in so much grandeur? We meander mindlessly throughout the packed crowds until daylight runs out.

Because we have waited too long, hunger obliterates any chance of rational judgment and we make an ill-conceived choice for dinner (all the charming restaurants are supremely packed) and we end up in a kind of dismal "mini-mall." Plastic plants abound on our second floor balcony table and though it is bustling with patrons our dinners prove less, much less, than mediocre. (Courtney cross examines me about my uneaten choice: "What were you thinking ordering a shrimp cocktail this far from the ocean … in Central Ecuador!!!?" *Well, I could recognize it on the menu!*)

We step back out onto the now dark streets.

The blanket of nightfall brings with it, for the first time on the trip (or any trip for that matter) a deep sense of fear, despite the heavy presence of *La Policía*. The police patrols are roaming the area on foot in groups of three and four officers in yellow jackets (the necessity of that in itself makes me wonder). I'm not sure why or if my sudden sense of alarm is justified.

---

* Appropriately this *Plaza de la Independencia* was named for just that 1809 occasion: King Ferdinand of Spain was deposed by Napoleon Bonaparte whereby Quito rebels seized upon this opportunity to take back their city from Spain.

We had been warned repeatedly to beware of the street crime in Quito and this certainly plays upon my perception—plus the fact that some of Carly's co-workers had been robbed by knifepoint here.

But some kind of metamorphosis seems to transpire once it gets dark; I'm suddenly, instinctively overwhelmed with the urgent sensation: ***we need to get out of here***.

It didn't help that earlier, as I was walking brusquely on a dimly lit walkway— ever looking upwards at the looming hillsides—I failed to perceive a metal traffic bumper. Bam! I had a head-on (well, solar plexus-on) collision and went flying through the air with the greatest ill-ease. With no time to catch myself, I hit the concrete full force. Major thud! *Oh no, this could be really serious,* I'm thinking. For some time I lay there, assessing my physical self, body part by body part, relieved not to detect any sickening, dull-throbbing injuries (as in a broken bone). I was astonished to walk away with only a slightly sprained ankle! (My stunning recovery greatly under-appreciated by my youthful daughters, though I tried hard to impress upon them my supreme agility! *They were having none of it.* Bah!)

Ambulant once again, my thoughts wandered back to the lone woman sitting on a park bench, a shopping bag at her side, who impassively observed my entire acrobatic feat *directly* three feet in front of her. She never stirred, not even slightly. Were my theatrics so mundane, so *aburrido* (boring) as to not stimulate any kind of response? Perhaps the bench is a prime viewing spot for continually tumbling gringas?

But now we need to get out of here. It's dark, I'm limping, and we can't find a taxi to save our lives. We decide to walk *away* from the plaza to find a busy thoroughfare in order to hail a taxi; but the further we walk from the square the scarier the scene gets. The characters I see emerging all about are unnerving: lone men in black leather and chains, unsavory looking strangers huddled in alleyways, groups of teens projecting an air of malice. We turn this way and that, repeatedly dead-ending in our quest. Speeding up and becoming somewhat erratic, we soon begin *to race* up one hill and down the other. Yikes. I'm feeling more and more like I'm in a carnivalesque nightmare. Carly sticks her arm out several times in an attempt to catch the notice of any speeding away taxi—to no avail. I'm constantly checking out the people around us, hoping to see the wholesome world of families out and about, only to see a semblance of the underworld out and about.

Seriously spooked, we decide *we'd better turn around* and head back toward the square.' Finally, with a great deal of relief, we chance upon one lone, available taxi. (Taxi defined as an old, battered compact with a sign in the window, albeit, a sign of a "safe taxi" company that's recommended by our guide book.) It is with *immeasurable relief* when we settle into that car for the long ride back to the airport. (Although it is kind of odd that our unforthcoming, somber driver has an equally silent friend riding next to him in the front seat. Neither will talk nor respond to our amiable chatter. *Are we in fact finally safe?*)

Well, yes, the non-speaking friend is dropped off after a few miles; we make it back safely, on time, full circle. Living to be foolish another day. Another trip.

---

*   2012: Alas, I came across a Frommers tour book recommendation **never to stray away from this Plaza at night**.

Carly's Ecuador Summary—August 2009

Wow it is so strange being home, I feel like I've been gone forever. My brain hasn't adjusted yet. As I was driving down the street and saw a person walking, my mind instantly recognized her as an indigenous woman going to the market. I feel so blessed for the enriching experience I had teaching and traveling in Ecuador. But, I think I'm experiencing for the first time reverse culture shock ... and strangely enough I've been gone for much longer before! It was so refreshing being away from the sensational media ... it is unsettling coming back to it, being bombarded with non-important information distracting us from truly important things going on in the world. On the other hand, I'm so appreciative of the Pacific Northwest. The wide open spaces, fresh air, gorgeous mountains and cities, laws that people mostly abide by, seatbelts, the non-electric showers, the organization and resources we have ... Yakima and my home looks like a beautiful, organized, luxurious clean oasis. Everyone always talks about how amazing the land is in Ecuador, but on every hike I went on I just kept thinking "the land in the Pacific Northwest is much more beautiful without scary bugs that can kill you!" The more I travel the more I realize how we are so spoiled here; it makes me feel so grateful and so sick at the same time. It is shocking to realize the drastically different life I have from my Ecuadorian students and my host family. I struggle with these differences—why do I have enough to eat and all the opportunities in the world and they don't, just by being born in a different place? I appreciate so much more all the resources I have here as a teacher (even though it still isn't adequate) but compared to Ecuador my students and I are rich with abundance. However, I feel the lack of cultural richness here ... it is so colorful and alive in Ecuador. If only my students in the mountains of *Huayrapungo* had the opportunities of education and enough food and proper medical care, their lives could be far superior to mine, living deeply spiritual lives with close ties to their families and the Earth. So, this is what my mind is thinking about now ... I'm very overwhelmed, contemplative, grateful, and sad all at the same time. I can't stand to turn on the TV or even read the newspaper because it is all too much and frustrating. It was so nice being focused on my duty and job in Ecuador, not thinking about all the problems in the world and being so frustrated at the state it is in now. But I know I have an important role here in Yakima as an educator and I'm excited and nervous that my old life begins anew in a very short amount of time.

I benefit much more than my students, as I learn and grow as a person and as an educator.

Mucho amor y besos safe back in Yakima!!

~Carlita

Safely home, standing outside on my patio, I look southward from Yakima and imagine all those thriving, colorful, music-filled plazas; people still dancing, still celebrating the parade of life, stretching all the way from Mexico to Panama to the tip of the South American continent.

Ahhhh, how beautiful.

Acknowledgments

Many thanks to Christen Cook for her incredible hard work and valuable contribution. To Martha Goudey for her assistance as well as inspiring me to go on, and to Wendy Warren as a selfless cheerleader. To my sisters Ginger, Jeanne and Mary Jane for their love and support—Jeanne (who put in the most time), your unwavering encouragement, belief and laughter always sustained me. And my immediate family, kind enough to tolerate infinite re-readings.

Sources

1. Seattle Weather July 29, 2009. http://en.wikipedia.org/wiki/2009-PacificNorthwest-heat-wave (accessed October 9, 2009)
2. Reggaetón. 2012. http://en.wikipedia.org/wiki/Reggaeton (accessed October 29, 2012)
3. Harpy Eagle. 2012. http://en.wikipedia.org/wiki/Harpy-eagle (accessed September 8, 2012
4. Wildlife Conservation Society wcs.org (http://www.wcs.org/saving-wildlife/birds/andean-condor.aspx
5. ProtectingEcuadorianDryForest,proforestfoundationorg.blogspot.com
6. exploringecuador.com Antonio Fresco y Catálogo del Museo del Banco Central del Ecuador Sala de Arquelogia
7. As quoted in Carroll, Sean B. *Remarkable Creatures* (Boston: Houghton Mifflin 2009), p. 34
8. Shah, Tahir. *The Trail of Feathers* (Great Britain: Weidenfeld & Nicolson, 2001) p. 112
9. http://www.ecuadorexplorer.com and tours-unlimited
10. Polla, Mario. *Peru.* A.B.A. Milan, trans. (Italy: White Star S.p.A.: 2003, 2006), p. 116
11. http://pum.princeton.edu/pumconference/papers/1-cerrutti.pdf, June 2003.
12. World Carbon Emissions: United States Energy Information Administration; Environmental Protection Agency (Keystone emissions). *New York Times*, April 24, 2014
13. http://www.patagonia.com/us/patagonia.go?assetid=2387, Betsy Taylor, 2004
14. Hemingway, Ernest. *Vanity Fair* October 2011, p. 284 (Original quote from Letters of Ernest Hemingway (February 14, 1922): Volume 1, 1907-1922, edited by Sandra Spanier and Robert W. Trogden. Cambridge University Press
15. Rasley, Jeff. *Bringing Progress to Paradise* (San Francisco: Red Wheel/Weiser, 2010), p. 13
16. Hoffman, Carl. *Lunatic Express* (New York: Crown Publishing Group, 2010), pp. 271-273
17. Leaming, Linda. *Married to Bhutan* (Carlsbad, CA: Hay House Inc., 2011), pp. 157-158

18. Szotek, Mark. *Interview with Dr. Jane Goodall.* Special to Mongabay, April 12, 2010 (http://news.mongabay.com)
19. Furst, Peter T. *Hallucinogens and Culture.* 1976 p.15 (http://www.erowid. org)
20. Richard Evans Schultes *Iconography of New World Plant Hallucinogens* New World Hallucinogens. William L. Brown Center. p. 81 (wlbcenter. org/Schultes%20Publications/Arnoldia41_3_1981.pdf)
21. Letcher, Andy. *Shroom* (New York: HarperCollins Publishers, 2006), p. 140 (Doctorate in religious/cultural studies from King Alfred's College, Winchester and doctorate in ecology from Oxford University)
22. Sting (Gordon Sumner). *Broken Music* (New York: Random House Publishing, 2005), p. 61
23. Tayler, Jill Bolte. *My Stroke of Insight* (New York: Plume Printing Penguin Group, 2006), pp. 41, 49
24. Miller, Arthur I. Professor of history and philosophy of science University College London, Jan. 2006 (http://www.nytimes.com)
25. Howe, Michael J.A. Howe. Professor of psychology at the University of Exeter. *Genius Explained.* Cambridge University Press, 1999, pp. 9, 10
26. Chomskey, Noam. *Discover Magazine* November 2011, p. 67
27. Blackenship, Judy. *Cañar* (Austin: The University of Texas Press, 2005), p. 124
28. Ibid., p. 23
29. Hour of the Wolf. 2013. http://www.tcm.com/this-month/ article/235825%7CO/Hour-of-the-Wolf.hyml